TEACH
YOURSELF
TO
MEDITATE

Further information on courses, retreats, books and tapes
by Eric Harrison can be obtained by contacting:

PERTH MEDITATION CENTRE
PO Box 1019, Subiaco WA 6904, Australia
Phone: (08) 9381 4877
Email: perthmed@global.net.au

Perth Meditation Centre offers:
- Meditation courses
(basic, intermediate and advanced levels)
- Workshops
- Seminars
- Retreats
- Private and telephone consultations
- Group Sittings

Perth Meditation Centre also sells:
- Books
- Tapes and CDs by Eric Harrison
(The new book *Meditation and Healing* is
due for publication in 1999.)

TEACH
YOURSELF
TO
MEDITATE
~ SECOND EDITION ~

Eric Harrison

SIMON & SCHUSTER
AUSTRALIA

TEACH YOURSELF TO MEDITATE (SECOND EDITION)

First published in Australia in 1998 by
Simon & Schuster Australia
20 Barcoo Street, East Roseville NSW 2069

A Viacom Company
Sydney   New York   London   Toronto   Tokyo   Singapore

National Library of Australia
Cataloguing-in-Publication data

Harrison, Eric.
   Teach yourself to meditate.

   2nd ed.
   Includes index.
   ISBN 0 7318 0738 3.

   1. Meditation. 2. Self-actualization (Psychology).
   I. Title.

158.12

Internal design: Siobhan O'Connor
Typeset in 10.5/14 pt Berkeley Book
Printed in Australia by Griffin Press

10 9 8 7 6 5 4 3 2

Contents

Introduction

Meditation is surprisingly simple. The principles and instructions are easy enough for a child to understand. When I teach meditation, people often say 'Is that all? There must be more to it.' In fact, meditation works because of its simplicity. If you can persuade your mind to do something simple, you automatically relax and the mind becomes clearer.

Paradoxically, it can be difficult to be simple. By choice or habit, we prefer to be mentally busy. We like to juggle many thoughts at once in the mind. We habitually think and worry, and usually think and worry too much. Useful as thinking seems to be, it burns a lot of energy and we become exhausted. As a result, we neither relax well nor think well. Our health often suffers and we don't enjoy life.

Thinking is a kind of 'doing'. By thinking, we are usually trying to sort something out. Meditation, however, is a deliberate 'not doing'. It is an intelligent laziness. We do our best to do as little as possible. By meditating, we shift from 'doing' to just 'being'. Once we stop trying to 'do' something, the body and mind relax naturally.

But how do we stop thinking? Trying to 'blank out' thoughts is usually a vain endeavour. Thoughts are always around, but we don't need to be at their mercy. Just as an antelope can live safely in the company of predators, so we can learn to escape thoughts at will. The strategy is simple and natural. All we have to do is shift from thinking to sensing.

Whenever we observe the sensations of the present — sight, sound, smell, taste or touch — our thoughts fade into the background. If you chose, right now, to listen carefully to the sounds around you for thirty seconds, you would find that other thoughts would vanish. Within a minute, you would feel your body relaxing.

This is the secret formula: to relax, be sensual. Shepherd the mind into the sense world. Taste the coffee, enjoy the evening clouds, sense your own body as you walk. Just focus more deeply than usual and the thoughts will fade into the background.

Most of us know this anyway. We choose to relax by doing sensual things: eating or drinking, listening to music, walking in the park. By doing so, we also leave behind our thoughts of the past and future — where most of our worries are — and enter the present moment. This is where meditation starts.

At first glance, meditation does not seem simple at all. There are, after all, thousands of different techniques with apparently different goals. Many are described in obscure, mystical language. Yet they all have a common core: relax the body and calm the mind. This is the starting point for virtually all techniques. They diverge after that.

Even the basic instructions tend to be similar. You pay attention to one thing (which we call the 'meditation object') and learn to let other thoughts and sensations pass by in the background. Meditation is based on these two skills: focusing on one thing — usually an object from the sense world — and detaching from, or 'just watching', all the rest.

The main difference between traditions is in the object upon which they choose to focus. Christian and New Age practices often focus on God, or a beautiful idea or image. Buddhist or Hindu groups are more earthy. They commonly focus on the breath or the body, or sounds or other sense objects. There are thousands of different possible meditation objects. It is the depth of focus, however, not the object itself, that matters. Deep focus on a twig, for example, will work better than shallow contemplation of a beautiful idea.

Meditation puts words in the background and, as a result, people often feel you should not talk about the experience. Consequently, meditators are often rather vague and inarticulate about what they do. Some schools encourage this mindless, semi-hypnotic, attitude to make their students dependent on them.

I found even my own teachers unable or unwilling to answer my questions. I would ask, 'How does meditation work? What happens physically and mentally? What are the best techniques?' Their usual response was 'Do it and find out.' I found, however, that if I analysed the process and discussed it with others, my meditation improved.

Although meditation is a non-verbal state, it is still very useful to think about it afterwards. So, when I started to teach, I tried to explain the process as clearly as possible and with a minimum of jargon. I wanted my students to know exactly what they were doing, so they could do it better. I became the kind of teacher I wanted to meet twenty-eight years ago.

How I Became a Teacher

For the past eleven years, teaching meditation has been my full-time occupation. (This doesn't stop people from asking me if I have a *real* job as well.) Full-time Western meditation teachers who are not monks or nuns are quite rare, but we do exist. I met my peers in 1993 and 1995 at conferences in San Francisco, and found we had a lot in common.

Most of us are in our forties or fifties (because it takes that long to get a handle on the mind's tricks). We typically spent years on the hippie trail in Asia in the early 1970s, and trained in a Buddhist or Hindu tradition. In those days, there was nowhere else you could learn meditation.

I left New Zealand at the age of twenty and spent four years travelling through Australia and Asia. Meditation came easily to me. I developed my own methods for relaxing the body and clearing the mind, which I eventually found were very like the Buddhist methods.

I started training formally in 1975 and developed a passion for ten-day intensive retreats in the Burmese tradition. By 1983, I was wanting more. So, for three years, I studied with Western teachers in the Kagyu lineage of Tibetan Buddhism. This culminated in a seven-month retreat at a meditation centre in the South Island of New Zealand. For most of those seven months, I lived in a tiny, unheated hut high on a mountainside. I would see no one all week except for Tuesdays. On that day, I would collect my week's food and visit my girlfriend in the adjacent hut.

I loved the months of solitude. I could feel the old self dying and the new one emerging. It was a powerful and inexorable process. All I had to do was watch it unfold. Although I did little else but sit, walk, cook and sleep, they were the richest months of my life. I was not bored for a moment. I could have stayed there much longer if it wasn't so cold! In the depths of the winter, I finally had to leave.

Reluctantly, I returned to my little farm in the sunny north. I was part of the 'back-to-the-land' movement of the 1970s. For eight years, I had built houses, planted trees, grown fruit and vegetables, tended bees and helped all my friends to do the same. I made a living by writing local histories and doing wildlife research and a little schoolteaching.

After my long retreat, that lifestyle no longer appealed to me. My teachers had suggested I start teaching meditation. There were few possibilities in New Zealand so, on my thirty-sixth birthday, I returned to Australia.

After revisiting old haunts in Sydney and the eastern states, I finished up in Perth on the west coast. My first class had twelve people and was held in a local learning centre. We could hear the shouts of the children at the creche, people gossiping at reception through the closed door and various dramas unfolding along the corridors as we tried to meditate. This is what we euphemistically call 'meditation in daily life'.

Fortunately, Perth seemed to need a meditation teacher. My work grew rapidly. Soon I was teaching four terms a year, with twelve courses each term, to about 1200 people a year. That pattern has continued for the past ten years.

Initially, I taught at civic centres, universities, schools, government offices, prisons and from my home. The surroundings were often far from perfect. I did not enjoy shifting tables and setting up chairs in unlovely, multipurpose rooms before each class. In 1990, I dropped the outside work and opened up the Perth Meditation Centre.

The centre was in West Perth, just a kilometre from the heart of the city. Across the road was Kings Park, 200 hectares of magnificent natural bush with escarpment views over the Swan River. We often used the park for walking meditations.

People coming to classes would go up two flights of stairs, past the offices of Fairfax Newspapers and the Mineral Mapping Agency. The centre occupied the top floor. It was simply furnished with jungles of plant life in the corners.

The main teaching room was spacious and airy, with natural light and views of the sky coming through windows on three sides. Although we could still hear the traffic, it was an unusually beautiful space to find in the heart of office-land. The room was very suitable for a class of twenty, yet at times we squeezed in more than a hundred people for public talks or workshops.

Over the years, I led hundreds of workshops as well as the regular courses. I gave hundreds of talks and led about forty retreats over the decade. I also sponsored the visits to Perth of Western teachers from the United States, Canada and New Zealand. I became a businessman as well as a meditation teacher worrying, as all businessmen do, about the overheads. My life was as busy as that of my students.

I had descended from the mountains of New Zealand to the marketplace in Perth. Without consciously planning it, I realised this had always been my goal. Much as I loved my time in retreat, it still had an escapist and hermit-like quality to it. I was never going to be a monk, so I knew I had to weave my meditation into a lifestyle I could sustain. As a teacher, I wanted to teach meditation where people needed it, in the midst of their busy lives.

I didn't want people to feel they had to withdraw into the woods in order to meditate. My students soon realise that meditating doesn't need perfect solitude. Within a week or two of classes, they find themselves meditating well in an office block in a busy part of town. They gradually learn to do the same at home, with the sounds of the traffic outside and the television and the kids down the hall.

In late 1997, when its building was under threat of demolition, I shifted the centre to the adjacent suburb of Subiaco where I live. The new centre is the same size, and as bright and spacious as the old one. The shift, however, brings a change in atmosphere. Unlike West Perth, Subiaco has a lively night scene. It has a 'cappuccino strip' plus many bars and theatres. There are twenty-five cafes and eating houses within 500 metres of the new centre! This is proving good for our social life and bad for our midlife waistlines.

How To Use This Book

This book contains all the exercises and explanations I give in my basic meditation course (I teach intermediate and advanced levels as well). If you can't come to my classes, this book should give you all you need to teach yourself. Most chapters mimic the way I teach a class. They start with the explanation of a theme and finish with a meditation exercise or two.

Some meditations are more useful than others. This may not be obvious, since they all require about the same number of words to explain them. You don't need to try out all the fifty or so meditations in this book. You could just do these four: the breath meditations (page 32), body scan (page 51), awareness (page 61) and mantra (page 68). You would be in good company. These four practices, or some variant of them, are the most popular in the world. They are easy to do immediately, but are also capable of infinite refinement.

These four practices are also good mixers. They combine well with other practices. For example, you can meditate on the breath while also listening to sounds and saying an affirmation. You can scan the body while doing a visualisation, too. Some practices are limited in scope, but others take you a long way. These four practices all have great potential. They all possess benefits that may be far from obvious at first glance.

I don't expect my students to practice every meditation. I lay out the smorgasbord and they choose what suits them. Nonetheless, by sampling a variety, they understand the overall principles better. This gives them more flexibility and allows them to be creative. I find most students eventually shape their practice to suit themselves. This is how it should be. The instructions I give in this book are just templates with which you can experiment.

It may reassure you to know that I do most of the meditations in this book as a matter of habit. I don't teach any practice that I don't do myself. These meditations have all been well tested by me and by my students, and I know their value. No meditation here has been 'cut-and-pasted' from someone else's book because I thought it looked useful.

Few of the ideas in this book are my own. Millions of people have meditated before me, and thousands have shared what they know. I even find it hard to regard this book as 'mine'. All the meditation exercises here were being used 2000 years ago. I have just put old wine into new bottles.

If you read this book and just 'imagine' doing the exercises, you will understand, in words, what meditation is about. If you try out two or three of them more deliberately, however, you will know it in your flesh and bones. Usually you need to do a meditation at least four times to engrave it in consciousness.

Sprinkled through the text are 'spot' meditations. You can do these wherever an opportunity presents itself — at traffic lights, in queues, walking the dog or while doing housework. These are not designed to relax you to the point of sleep. They just strip off the top 20 per cent of tension and wind down the mental chatter. Often they are just short forms of the standard meditations. If you want to be relaxed right through the day, and not just when you formally meditate, try out these exercises.

This book is a ready-mix kit. You just add time. If you read this book and do those exercises that appeal to you, you will both understand what meditation is, and know how to do it. If you invest fifteen minutes a day, five days a week, for two months, you will be more relaxed, aware, healthy and in tune with yourself. For a total of ten hours practice, you can develop a skill that may permanently benefit the rest of your life. Have fun!

Eric Harrison, 1998
Perth, Western Australia

CHAPTER I

What Is Meditation?

This chapter explains meditation in a nutshell — what meditation is like, the general principles behind it, how to do it, what happens when you meditate and how to spread your practice throughout the day. The details are given more fully in later chapters.

What Is Meditation Like?

When you meditate, you are both relaxed and alert. It is a state of 'calm awareness'. The mind is not actively thinking. Meditation is a passive, but watchful, state. You are conserving, not burning, energy. You are 'being' rather than 'doing'.

Sometimes when you meditate, your body is almost asleep. At other times, you can be relaxed and alert with your eyes open, and your body moving. Tai Chi and yoga, for example, can relax the body and clear the mind just as effectively as sitting cross-legged on the floor. When you recognise this state of mind, you can be very flexible about how you meditate. You no longer have to sit still, with your eyes closed and in a quiet place. Here are some examples.

You can meditate on objects of beauty

Sometimes I meditate by going bush. My 'backyard' is Kings Park, which is 200 hectares of bushland between my home in Subiaco and the Swan River. Often, I enter the park with my head full of thoughts, mentally writing this book as I walk. The scene is too lovely, however, to ignore. It is time to put thoughts aside for a while. It is spring, the season of wildflowers. The rainbow-coloured parrots are feeding on the bottlebrush flowers, the air is rich with scent and the afternoon sun shines on the white bark of the gum trees.

The wildflowers are very seductive. Like babies and cats, they demand your attention. Soon I find myself examining a blossoming bush. Some flowers are in full bloom, some are half-opened. Others are already drying out and decaying, but all are perfect. An ant is running up the stem, and the broken strands of a cobweb waft on the still air.

The thoughts and concerns I brought into the park have slipped away. I am in a different time and space. I am both relaxed and alert. This is meditation — a state in which my mind is quiet and I am alive to the sensations of the moment. When I turn away from the flowers, my mind is clear of other thoughts.

You can also meditate by consciously doing a simple activity

'I meditate at work two or three times a day,' says a bank manager. 'At home, I relax by listening to music, but I can't do that at work. So I have a glass of water instead.'

The water cooler is 30 metres down a corridor. When the bank manager stands up, she mentally leaves all the work on her desk. Going down the corridor, she breathes easily and consciously feels her body moving. She feels the touch of the plastic cup, listens to the trickle of the water, tastes each sip slowly and hears the cup fall into the bin. Then she walks back. Only when she reaches her desk, does she mentally return to work.

You don't even have to escape your thoughts

One student prefers to 'just watch' them come and go, with detachment. 'I don't try to block anything,' he said. 'Sometimes I even invite all the thoughts to come at once. I imagine them to be like garbage floating down a river. If I find I'm holding a thought, I throw it back in, and let the river carry it away.'

Meditation can be quite energetic

'I meditate while swimming,' says another student. 'I focus on each breath, making it full and rhythmic, and synchronising it with my arms. If I am still thinking too much, I also chant a mantra or an affirmation to blow the words away.' Sometimes, she watches the explosion of bubbles as well. 'Swimming used to be so boring,' she said, 'but now I come out of the pool feeling great.'

You can focus on the sensations around you at random

'I just try to be in the present,' said another student. 'My husband and I go camping in the Kimberley every two or three years, but this was our best holiday ever — especially in the evenings. I would watch the shadows creeping across the landscape, watch the smoke rising from the barbecue and hear the food cooking. I would listen to the birds and the sound of the wind in the trees. I would consciously take in one sensation after another.'

Meditation doesn't always have to be pleasant

'I meditate best with pain,' said a student with cancer. 'It often becomes so intense, I have to drop everything else, lie down and focus on it. First I notice my whole body is rigid, trying to avoid the pain. So I scan it from top to bottom, telling myself, "It's okay to let go now."

'Then I go into the pain itself. I stop fighting, and let my mind sink into it. I caress the pain with my breathing. I watch the pain ache and pulse. I tell myself, "It is just sensation," and I let my fears go. I often get very peaceful, and sometimes I go to sleep. The pain always fades when I meditate.'

A meditation can literally be just a few seconds long

'I was waiting to pick up my child outside the school,' said one woman. 'He was late as usual, and I felt annoyed and tired. So I meditated. I decided to watch the raindrops running down the windscreen. It was very soothing. I was sorry to stop when my son turned up.'

You can meditate formally

Another student prefers to meditate formally, for up to an hour at a time. 'As I count the breaths, I feel the body becoming heavy, and numb. Each time I breathe out, I drop everything — thoughts, tensions, the lot. I lose myself into the breath. I just love that space between outbreath and inbreath. It seems a pity to breathe and disturb it.

'Then I go into the space between the heartbeats. My body feels like it is dissolving. Thoughts still go by, but they don't bother me at all. I feel so peaceful, I can't imagine anything better.'

Being Relaxed and Alert

A question I often face is: 'What is the difference between relaxation and meditation?' People rightly suspect that meditation is more than just being relaxed.

Meditation is a calm and alert state of mind. It is when the body is relaxed and the mind is focused. Relaxation, on the other hand, is when the mind wanders. It may drift between thought and fantasy and sleepiness. Relaxation is usually a pleasant state, but it is unstable, out of control and often contaminated by thought. It rarely becomes as still and clear as a good meditation.

We are most likely to be relaxed and alert when we pay attention to something we enjoy. In other words, something attracts us and we focus on it. We may be in this state while:

• listening to music;
• watching birds play in the backyard;
• doing yoga, or indeed any exercise, with awareness;
• having a shower;
• eating a peach;
• arranging flowers; or
• lying in bed, listening to the wind and the rain.

One woman told me: 'When my kids were little, I would lie on the couch in the afternoon to rest. My eyes were closed and my body was resting, but I stayed awake. I kept track of the kids by listening to the sounds they made.' She was relaxed, but her mind was still alert. She was focusing on sound.

Meditation is a balancing act between relaxation and alertness. We may be relaxed, but not very alert. Or we may be alert, but physically tight. Usually our anxieties keep us wired up, so we need to relax more. At other times, we are half asleep and need to wake the mind up. With fine-tuning and practice, we can achieve the best of both worlds: a meditator can relax deeply *and* stay mentally clear at the same time.

You could say that meditation is the art of falling asleep and staying awake simultaneously. Usually when the body falls asleep, the mind follows. In meditation, however, you break that linkage. You let the body go to sleep, but keep the mind awake.

This takes a while to learn. It usually happens in two stages. It is said 'First calm the mind, then wake it up.' In the first stage of meditation, you learn to relax. Once you succeed in letting thoughts go, the body relaxes rapidly. Now, however, you have another problem.

As you approach the sleep state, you start to lose control. Your mind wanders, the head nods and you can't remember what you are doing. This is where stage two starts. You learn to keep the mind awake while the body goes to sleep.

Early in a course, students often relax well, but err on the side of drowsiness. They master stage one, but struggle with stage two. Yet even to manage stage one is quite good. It is no small task to calm down an overactive mind. For some people, it is quite an achievement to be nodding off, in a chair, in a roomful of strangers. Gradually, as the weeks pass, they incorporate stage two—they learn to stay alert as their bodies relax. This is meditation.

The Art of Relaxing Quickly and Consciously

Often we can be relaxed and alert without needing to meditate at all. This state is quite common. It may occur while stroking a cat or having a cup of tea on the verandah. We may be absorbed in craft work or a good book, or gardening or preparing a meal.

Yet these peaceful moments don't come as often as we would like. Simply doing what we like is no guarantee of peace. We can't just stroke the cat, or walk in the park, and immediately hope to feel good. If we are upset, the mind will ramble and fuss whatever we do. We can walk right through the park and be aware of nothing but our thoughts and obsessions. We all have strategies to relax, but for many of us they are often slow and ineffective.

Meditation, in contrast, is fast. It is the art of relaxing quickly and consciously, whenever you want to and in any circumstances. Some people may take five hours to wind down after a demanding day at work. A meditator, however, can come home, shed the thoughts of the day and relax the body to the point of sleep in five minutes.

So what makes meditation so efficient? First, when we are meditating, we are focused. Secondly, we are predominately sensing, rather than thinking. Thirdly, we are in the present.

The Mind Is Focused

In all the meditations and examples above, the mind was focused on something. People were meditating on wildflowers, a cup of water, pain, shoulders, sounds or their breathing. Sometimes they stayed with one object for a long time; at other times, their mind shifted amongst different sensations. The common thread is that they all deliberately focused on *something*.

When the mind drifts aimlessly from one concern to another, it becomes exhausted and confused, and we feel bad. A wandering mind may seem pleasant at first, but it is out of control and unpredictable. It usually drifts up into thought, or down into sleep. A mind that is settled on one thing, however, or that is simply absorbing the sensations of the moment, is happy ... and the body responds. It is almost as if it says, 'There is obviously no emergency here. I can relax now.'

This is one of the basic principles of meditation: if you want to relax, then don't simply allow your mind to drift. Focus on something.

Sensing Rather Than Thinking

It is very hard suddenly to stop thinking. To 'take our mind off things', we often try to blank out or go into a vague mental space. We watch television or read the newspaper absentmindedly. Many people do, in fact, meditate to induce this numb, dull, flat state of mind — it can be peaceful. Meditation, however, is much more than this state of mild depression.

In meditation, we don't try to smother the words—we divert our attention away from them. We shift from thinking to sensing. We deliberately focus on something sensual. Most meditation objects are things in the sense world — the breath, pain, sounds, flowers, light. These are much simpler for the mind to process than the complexity of thought, so we relax.

Our mental activity changes dramatically when we shift from thinking to sensing. *Thinking* is busy and burns a lot of energy. It is proactive and involves words and concepts of past and future. Thinking usually feels 'tight' and is powered by underlying fear, anger or desire. It is exciting, but it is also exhausting. The brain emits the fast arrhythmic *beta* brainwaves when we think.

Sensing, however, is quite the opposite. Sensing is passive. It requires much less energy than thinking, so we relax. It doesn't involve words or concepts of the past and future. It is emotionally more 'loose' and fluid. When sensing, or relaxing, the brain emits the slower and more rhythmic *alpha* brainwaves.

Being in the Present

We usually spend very little time in the present. If we look at what is happening in our minds, most of it relates to the past or future. We just check into the sense world occasionally, so we don't bump into doors or get killed crossing the road.

Yet when we are relaxed, or meditating, we are present. When we are tasting food or watching our breath,the past and future temporarily vanish. This is an enormous relief. Most of our anxieties relate to past and future. We can escape them by entering the present moment fully. And we often find the present is a lovely space, full of light, colour and beauty that we miss if we are lost in thought.

If we think a lot about the past and future, we are bound to be unhappy to some degree. Both are frustratingly beyond our control and contain many unresolvable problems. If we want to be happy, trying to fix up the past or manipulate the future is certainly not the way to go about it.

As adults, we tend to carry the burden of our years and our personal history. The effortless joy of childhood seems far away. Yet we can recapture that joy if we can drop fully into the present — if only for a few seconds or minutes at a time.

The pleasure doesn't last forever. It never did (even though we didn't realise that when we were young). It can, however, be just as perfect as it ever was. To put it another way, the more time we spend in the present moment, in touch with the sense world, the more we enjoy life. Conversely, the more we live in the past and future, the more anxious we become.

How to Meditate

The basic instructions for most meditations are the same:

1. Relax the body.
2. Focus on one thing.
3. When the mind wanders, bring it back.
4. Let everything pass by.

In other words, you give the mind a simple task to do. You watch your breathing, or say an affirmation, or listen to the sounds around you. *This* is focusing. Sooner or later, you will notice that your attention has strayed. Without becoming annoyed with yourself, you return to the object.

It sounds like work — and indeed it is. We love to play with our thoughts — chasing the good ones, battling the bad. We don't want to give up our worries and fantasies, however frustrating they may be. Yet we can't relax unless we do. Loosening our grip on them can be quite hard work!

Focusing is the basic technique of almost all meditation. The term can be problematic for some people, who associate it with knitted brows and grim determination. For this reason, some teachers claim their practices do not involve focusing. But they do. There is always something central in the meditation upon which you focus.

Good focusing is joyful. The Indian word for it — *samadhi* — is a synonym for deep pleasure. When a child is absorbed in a toy, he is focused, sensing and in the present moment. This is enjoyable. It is healthy for the body and mind.

Focusing occurs naturally when something attracts us. It also a skill we can develop. It cannot be forced, but it can be encouraged. Focusing shouldn't be intense. A gentle curiosity is best. Eventually, the mind wants to focus because the resulting mind state is so pleasant.

What Happens When You Meditate?

In theory, you can focus on literally anything at all. In practice, however, most meditators at least start with the same object every time. Certain objects are extremely popular. They work very well for most people. Most of the world's millions of meditators use their breathing or their own body sensations, or perhaps a single, repeated word or phrase as their anchor.

So, what happens in a typical meditation? Normally, you would sit down in a quiet space. Most Westerners would use an upright, padded chair. This is comfortable, but also keeps the mind alert. If you are very tense, sitting in a reclining chair or lying on the bed may be better — but beware of falling asleep.

For instance, you may try to focus on the breath. You may try to count your breaths, up to ten repeatedly. Often the mind rebels at first. The unfinished business of the day usually crowds in as soon as you sit down. The first minute or two of a meditation is often quite scrappy. You try to shepherd the mind towards the breath, but the mind wants to go elsewhere. Eventually, the mind chatter fades and you actually start to *feel* the breath. You sense it rising and falling, or feel the body expanding and contracting. The breath comes into focus. You notice more detail than you did earlier.

Although you are focusing on the breath, the rest of the world doesn't vanish and you don't go blank. Thoughts still arise, a headache may remain. You still hear sounds outside and notice other sensations in the body. These need not distract you. You can notice them without losing the breath.

Yet, before you know it, some thought has enticed you away and you've abandoned the breath altogether. When you realise this, don't get annoyed. It is bound to happen. Now, however, you have the choice. You can either continue with the thought or you can drop it and return to the breath. If you drop it, you have a moment of liberation. You have cut loose from a thought that was probably stirring up your feelings and you return to the simplicity of the breath.

Unfortunately, being peaceful is not as exciting nor as emotionally charged as thinking. I know people who eagerly meditate waiting for something to happen. Or they may wait impatiently for the beautiful mind state they achieved a week ago. Meditation, however, is subtle, with few fireworks. Becoming peaceful is like developing an appreciation for clean water. You enjoy the feeling of your body and mind slowly settling. It is a state of wanting nothing and being happy with where you are.

Our meditation never seems perfect. The mind rarely sits still. It invariably oscillates between thoughts, the body, the breath and plain old unconsciousness. In a twenty-minute meditation, we may well be focused on the breath for only five minutes in total. Yet that is all you need. The meditation still works. That would be a 'good' meditation.

Just the effort to discard thoughts is enough. A few seconds or minutes of good focus is all you need to relax rapidly. To your surprise, you may find your head is starting to nod. Despite your mental chatter, you realise you have slowed down your metabolic rate and your body is sinking towards sleep.

Some meditations are 'messy' with lots of thoughts running through your mind. At other times, beautiful mind states and flashes of insight can arise. In time, deep peace, mental clarity, profound physical pleasure come so commonly that we start to take them for granted. Often they are quite brief — just flashes of sunlight in a cloudy sky. No state of mind, however lovely, stays forever. Whether a meditation is pleasant or not, you usually feel better for quite a while afterwards.

Expanding Your Practice

Most people treat meditation as something formal. It is something they do for maybe twenty or thirty minutes a day, rather like practising a musical instrument. Most would do exactly the same thing each day, using the same meditation object. This is where this book starts.

I begin by explaining how to meditate on the breath. This is our prototype. First you learn to relax somewhat, sitting in a quiet place, with eyes closed, focusing on your breathing. Then you branch out from here.

In time you learn to focus on different things. In subsequent chapters, I explain how to meditate on the body as a whole, on sounds, on visual objects, on affirmations and on their Asian equivalents, mantra.

These are all sense objects and they are the best foundation for meditation. These are the practices I teach in my Basic Meditation Course. Other objects can, however, also be used. I also train people to meditate on images, emotions, pain, concepts and on the quality of mind itself.

Similarly, you learn to meditate in many postures. You gradually learn to relax the body and clear the mind with your eyes open, while standing, while walking, while doing exercise or carrying out simple household activities. 'I really enjoy the ironing now,' said one of my students. It is a luxury to be able to meditate during boring lectures or meetings.

You learn to meditate in short bursts, many times a day. It only takes ten seconds, focusing deeply on something in the sense world, to extract yourself from thought. You can look at a pot plant or a tree outside your office window. You can give full attention to the next sip of tea. Ten seconds is all it takes to slow the brainwaves down.

Once you are clear on the principles, you have enormous freedom in how you apply them. You could meditate in a bank queue or while having a shower. You can meditate on a chocolate eclair or the sound of the air-conditioner. You can meditate for ten seconds or for an hour. Your metabolic rate could be high (while doing exercise, for example) or low (as you enter states close to sleep). At any time, you can switch into 'watching' mode — able to just 'watch' your thoughts and emotions pass, without reacting to them.

Eventually meditation ceases to be a formal exercise that you do for a few minutes each day. It becomes a quality of body and mind you can activate whenever you need it, in the space of just a few breaths.

SPOT MEDITATION: RED LIGHT

This exercise works best if you are running late, in a hurry and the traffic lights turn red just as you approach.

Instructions

- If you feel frustrated, smile at yourself.
- Relax: you have been given perhaps a whole minute to stop and do nothing.
- Take a deep sigh, lingering on the out breath.
- Let your body and mind slow down and relax.
- Let your face and belly soften.
- Take one whole minute to breathe softly.
- Be aware of excess tension in your body. How are you holding the steering wheel? Are your face and neck muscles tighter than they need to be?
- Gently shake yourself free, as you settle back into the seat.
- Look around you slowly.

The exercise finishes as the light turns green. Now devote all your attention to the task at hand: driving safely. And look forward to the next red light.

CHAPTER 2

Why Do People Meditate?

In February 1972, after three dramatic months in Indonesia, I was on the day ferry to Penang in Malaysia. I felt utterly confused. I didn't seem to know where I was going or why I was travelling. Although I tried to think it through, that just seemed to make it worse. I knew the only solution was to stop thinking for a while. So I promised myself three days free of thought.

Once in Penang, I picked up some fruit, bread and water, and caught the bus to the end of the road. I then walked beyond the last settlement around the coast. Dense jungle crowded the beaches, but small tracks allowed me to walk on for a few miles. I found a perfect little beach, about 200 metres long, with islands offshore and shade in the jungle. I stayed there two days and nights, sleeping on the sand in my cotton blanket under the stars.

While there, I meditated a lot. I would sit with eyes open, gently combing the tensions out of my body and brushing thoughts aside. Most of the time, however, I deliberately looked and listened and felt and tasted and smelt. When I felt myself succumbing to thought, I would look intently at a leaf or the activity of ants. I explored the jungle. I swam. I made sculptures from sand and jungle debris. I watched the changing light from dawn to dusk and felt the breeze move across my skin.

I still remember so many details of those two days: the golden, but gritty, quality of the sand, for example. I also remember the platoon of Australian soldiers who plunged out of the jungle and marched past me as I lay naked on the beach. Their day packs were the same as mine (I had bought mine in an army surplus store in Sydney).

By the second evening, I was completely content. My mind was back in my body and my body was again in touch with the earth. Without any actual thinking, the answers were clear. I walked out of there knowing where I was going and what it was all for. I went straight back to the city and boarded the boat to India.

Is Meditation Good for Everything?

People meditate for a multitude of reasons. In the episode above, I meditated to escape the mind chatter, to relax physically, to enjoy my surroundings, to gain inspiration and to make a decision.

Others meditate for quite different reasons. They seek better powers of concentration or improved sporting performance, or perhaps more creativity and lateral thinking. Some seek spiritual insight or self-awareness, or to purge the demons of the past. A huge number meditate for better health.

About a quarter of my students are referred to me by doctors. Thousands of scientific studies have confirmed the benefits of meditation, and this is now widely accepted in medical circles (this is expanded upon in chapter 12, pp. 88–95).

People often have a precise reason for meditating — to heal an illness or to study better, for example. They frequently get something different or more than they expect. They come for relief from insomnia and find their relationships improve. They come for hypertension and find peace and purpose in life. They come to cope with stress at work and, as a side effect, their headaches vanish or they can reduce their asthma medication.

The benefits of meditation ripple through everything that we do. They mean having more energy, being healthier, thinking and working more efficiently and enjoying life more. Being relaxed and alert is the mental equivalent of being fit and healthy. We sleep well, rise early and the freshness of morning seems to last all day. Our thoughts are more lucid and we feel 'on top of things'.

Meditation Is Not a Universal Panacea

Sometimes, meditation is promoted as the cure for everything, rather like those patent medicines of the nineteenth century or the latest potion in the health food stores. 'Meditation will help your insomnia, stomach cramps, poor memory, melancholy, PMT and self-esteem. Oh, yes, and your warts will disappear, too!'

Meditating, however, is like building good health. It takes time and effort, and rarely gives perfect results. Meditation is good, but it still can't turn straw into gold. Wonderful as it is, I do feel ashamed of the way some people promote it. Some New Age groups tout it as a magical and instantaneous route to boundless wealth, sexual vigour, power over others and physical immortality. (I am not exaggerating their claims!)

Meditation *can* have an element of self-hypnosis about it. Unfortunately, this can also mean self-deception. While it can be good to use positive thoughts and images to steer yourself towards an attainable goal, meditation won't work as a magical charm if you are aiming for the sky.

I knew a lady who had perfect faith that she would survive her breast cancer. Her faith was awe-inspiring. Although she was obviously and messily dying, there were no chinks in her mental armour. If you truly can 'create your own reality' through your thoughts, she would be alive today.

It is true that we can change our view of reality by changing our thoughts about it. Reality itself, however, can be stubborn. It often doesn't give a damn what we think. Meditation does work, but it is good to have your feet on the ground as well. Meditation is very valuable, but it does have limits.

Meditating to Relax

Each year, I get hundreds of phone calls about meditation. 'I need to meditate,' the caller will say, 'I'm stressed out' or 'I'm going through a hard time' or 'I can't sleep' or 'I'm having panic attacks.' After years of chronic stress, people lose their ability to relax. There are millions who require pills for a function as natural as sleeping.

Under ideal conditions, the body/mind tenses and relaxes regularly during the day. We rev up and slow down, roughly, on a ninety-minute cycle. Unfortunately, we tend to stubbornly fight this natural cycle. We try to stay revved up for sixteen hours, and get all our rest at night. We try to power through the low patches in the day, and grimly hang on to the highs.

This isn't natural, so we become exhausted beyond the point of recovery.

A Zen master, when asked the secret of his attainment, said, 'When hungry, I eat. When sleepy, I sleep.' On my seven-month retreat, I let myself sleep when I wanted to. By the end, I was sleeping five times a day, often for only fifteen minutes at a time. If we could relax whenever we were sleepy, or just take it easy when our energy dropped during the day, I think most of our health problems would vanish.

Meditation is sometimes called the art of conserving energy. We learn to use just the right amount of energy for the task at hand. When working, we just work. We don't burn extra energy thinking about yesterday and tomorrow as well. When we talk to a difficult person, we say just what is necessary and no more.

Thinking — and the emotions that drive it — exhausts the body and mind. Worrying will literally burn more kilojoules than manual labour. If you want to relax, do some bricklaying. It will be far more refreshing than sitting in a chair fretting ... and better for your back.

Fear, anger and desire release energy quickly into the bloodstream in case you need to do something physical. If we don't act, the valves remain open and the energy reserves leak away. When you are running on empty, the body processes suffer. You don't metabolise food well, breathe well, think well or move well. Because this feels so bad, you try to push on to cope with it. This means you can't even relax well, despite being exhausted.

Some people suffer only mild symptoms such as insomnia and digestive problems. Others, however, can be in constant states of extreme anxiety. Panic attacks, nervous breakdowns and physical collapse are very real dangers for them — just because they can't relax at all.

The body is very resilient. We can abuse it dreadfully and it still plods on. Years of push and exhaustion do, however, have their price. We get sick, we age more rapidly, we don't enjoy life much. Looking ahead, we just see more of the same, only worse. At some point, you say to yourself: 'I've got to learn to relax.' After years of neglect, relaxing becomes a priority.

Meditation often seems a 'spiritual' activity, but the path starts right here in the physical world. Everyone needs to relax. Everyone needs a good sleep. Meditation is the art of relaxing quickly and consciously, in any situation. First you learn to relax in a quiet place, with eyes closed.

Eventually, you can be relaxed while driving, eating or talking — even while having an argument. You no longer blow a fuse. You pace yourself. You relax at odd moments in the day and you relax fully at night.

Quality of Life

Our life suffers if we worry. No amount of money will buy us pleasure, let alone happiness, if our minds are too cluttered to take in that pleasure. If we discard unnecessary thought, however, we can make our lives rich again.

Monks and nuns are assumed to lead lives of deprivation: no sex, no entertainment, little food. In fact, they may be leading lives of refined sensuality. They have time to feel the morning air on their face, to watch the wind rustling through the trees, to feel the pleasure of their body moving.

Years ago, at the end of each teaching term, I used to have a meal with sixty to eighty meditators at a friend's restaurant. He said that, for us, he always prepared less food than usual. Since it was a smorgasbord, people could eat as much as they liked. Meditators, however, tend to taste their food. They know how their body feels and so they don't like to eat too much. The usual customers, on the other hand, would eat a lot. They would go back for a second or third plate because they were too mentally busy to enjoy the first.

When we drop the inner conversations, we enter a world rich in feeling and sensing. We can re-enter the mind state of a little child. Smells, tastes, sounds, sights and textures become more vivid and satisfying. We talk, but enjoy the food as well. We drive home from work, but still enjoy the sunset. We know what gives us real pleasure, and don't just blindly consume. A meditator is an epicure of simple things. For these reasons alone, meditators tend to be happier people.

Meditating for Clarity of Mind

If we feel stressed, the mind scatters. We try to think and do a dozen things at once, and we do none of them well. We become absentminded; we forget names; we lose our train of thought in a conversation; we walk into a room to get something and can't remember what it was.

Meditation trains us to pay attention to one thing at a time. We learn to focus without being distracted by the mental trivia and inner dialogues. We remember names, facts and details because we actually noticed them in the first place. Indeed, many university students come to my class to help them concentrate better.

Focusing has two aspects. First, we can see what we are looking at more clearly. The detail becomes obvious and we understand what we are observing. Secondly, by focusing, we shake off the distractions. This makes the mind more focused in the sense that it can see without other things getting in the way. With a uncluttered mind, we can detach from the trivia and see the big picture. We know what is happening, what is important and what we need to do.

Creativity, Lateral Thinking and Insight

'I get so many ideas in a meditation class,' said one visual artist, 'they last all week.' We normally think in words, and we steer those words actively. Useful as this is, it tends to block images and more subtle feelings.

As we relax, however, the words fade. The mind is closer to the dream state and is more receptive to imagery and feeling. Our 'thinking' becomes more lateral and associative. We see connections rather than 'think through' an issue. Patterns suddenly become clear and solutions are obvious. When we worry, we often can't see the forest for the trees. We get lost in minutiae. Meditation enables us to stand back and watch, rather like withdrawing to a mountain to survey the terrain below.

Insight can arise. This is a technical term. When the mind is clear and we are not trying to do anything, answers just pop up. These are moments when the lights go on. Sometimes these insights are quite trivial. As we relax, we suddenly remember that person's name. Or where we put the car keys. The deep part of the mind always knew these things. The surface static, however, needed to clear before the mind could deliver the message.

In the West, we value intellectual thought highly. We also like to shape our personalities by cultivating certain ideas. The Eastern way of self-knowledge, however, is not to think actively, but to listen within oneself. If the mind is still and clear, then insight, or our inner wisdom, can arise. We know as individuals who we are and what is going on. According to the Buddhists, this is the only truth worth having. Over the years, a meditator taps into that deep stream of inner wisdom — the things that you never realised the mind knew.

Meditating for Improved Performance

In the United States, many meditation teachers earn their living training sportspeople and stage performers. Such people realise that meditation gives them the edge they need for peak performance. They know it is not enough to just pump out the adrenalin.

Muhammad Ali used to say 'I float like a butterfly, sting like a bee.' Great dancers, tennis players and actors have a grace and ease in performance. They are relaxed. They use a lot of energy, but not too much all at once. They pace themselves. They use the right amount of energy for the task at hand, and relax well when they can. Good performance needs tension, but it has to be the right amount at the right time.

I once helped train a singer for a national competition. 'Sometimes I am too relaxed, or my build-up peaks too early,' she said. Her aria was so demanding, she couldn't give it a full-blown rehearsal more than three or four times a week. And she had to relax (i.e. remember to breathe) in the midst of it. She won the competition (after failing in previous years) and has now gone on to an international career.

Many of us have to perform in our work. We have to give a presentation or a talk; we go for a job interview; we have to do something exactly right, under pressure, with people watching us. Sometimes we pace ourselves well. Other times, we struggle through in a state of panic. Some people collapse and have to go on stress leave.

Musicians become too shaky to play. Singers lose their voice. Sportspeople become physically rigid or have to vomit before a game. I have worked with both kinds of performers—those near their peak, wanting to get better, and those who are struggling just to continue. I have now seen several sportspeople achieve their personal best through meditation, and seen many others (particularly musicians) just return to work.

Meditating for Self-Awareness and Therapy

Neurotic people tend to live in their heads. They don't even notice, for example, when they light another cigarette or eat another biscuit. Anorexics are obsessed with the idea, not the reality, of their bodies. Meditation brings us down to earth. It puts us in touch with the sensations of the body and what we are actually feeling. This is the raw data of self-awareness. It may not be comfortable, but it is who we are right now.

There are many bad or mediocre paths of inner growth. Many self-development books are based on a denial of reality. Even quite good spiritual or psychological disciplines can be escapist fantasies if nothing happens internally. The best test is to ask yourself: 'Does this match my experience? Or is it just words and fantasy and beliefs?'

Meditation is very practical. Things happen within minutes. The body chemistry changes and you can feel it. The mind becomes freer. You feel more content. The blind anger and irritability fade. You know you are doing something useful because it feels good. It may not be easy, but it has promise.

Relaxing has many degrees of depth. Relaxing loosens the tensions of the day. By loosening the mental control, our inner feelings may also surface. We may realise we are still upset by an argument from that morning or feel sad for no particular reason.

Deep relaxation can release the chronic in-built tension of years. The emotion that put your shoulder pain in place may surface. It may also throw up the buried memories and emotions that are behind it, allowing them to be acknowledged and cleared. In its own way, meditation covers exactly the same ground as any psychotherapy.

Spiritual Awakening

For the spiritual path, we need to clear the mind and listen. The Christian mystic Meister Ekhardt said we must become a space for God to enter into. We can't think our way to God. Grace only comes when the mind is open and receptive.

Many Christians come to my classes. They find when they try to pray, their minds are still contaminated with an endless parade of petty concerns. Meditation can weed these out, as they arise from moment to moment, so eventually a person has space to pray. It is said, 'When you master the small moments, the great moment is at hand.'

Buddhists, Christians and New Age people use different terminology, but the dynamic is the same. The Buddhists say: 'When the mind is clear, insight arises.' This is regarded as the inner wisdom of the psyche itself, or the 'buddhamind'. New Agers talk about contacting your 'higher power' or the 'spirit guides'.

Whether Christian, Buddhist, Hindu or New Age, meditators need to be clear of their usual self-orientated concerns. Ideally, they should be in a 'transpersonal' space, where they are still conscious and in control, but have little awareness of self. Meditation is the essential preparation for this state.

It may seem that a person aiming for spiritual awakening will meditate differently from someone trying to overcome insomnia. The ground rules, however, are the same for both. To succeed, both these types of meditator need to know how to be relaxed and alert, both in meditation and in daily life. Anything we do with our minds we do better if we meditate.

Meditation is like learning to drive a car. There are certain inescapable procedures we have to follow. Once we learn, however, it is up to us where we choose to drive.

SPOT MEDITATION: COUNTDOWN

This is a seven-breath meditation. You scan the body over seven breaths, counting down from the numbers seven to one as you go. You divide the body into seven stages from top to bottom, and imagine breathing through each part in turn. You shift from one stage to the next each time you breathe out.

Any place will do. Try it out in a supermarket queue or while walking or as a preliminary to any other meditation.

Instructions

- Loosen up your body. Consciously sit, stand or walk more comfortably.
- Take two or three deep breaths and sigh as you breathe out. Then let the breathing be normal.
- Scan the body over seven stages, counting from seven to one as you go. Spend one breath in each area:

Seven:	Scalp and forehead
Six:	The face and lower part of the head
Five:	Neck, throat and shoulders, arms and hands
Four:	Chest and back
Three:	Diaphragm and solar plexus
Two:	The belly
One:	The hips, legs and feet

Be gentle. It should be like touching each part of your body, giving it permission to let go. Or you can imagine you are caressing the body with the breath. Repeat the sequence as you wish.

Repeat this meditation as you wish. Or scan the body more slowly (i.e. three breaths to each area).

CHAPTER 3

Understanding Stress

When we say 'I'm under so much stress!', we imply that we are the victims of outer forces. Stress, however, is not beyond our control. The stress we feel is our fear or anger response to stimuli, preparing the body for fight-or-flight. Unfortunately, we usually blame the stimuli and as a result feel helpless. We rarely notice that we *can* change our response.

We usually try to ignore stress rather than face it. Although stress is uncomfortable, it is easy to block out temporarily. We can talk, eat, drink, work, watch television or take a pill. In doing so, we relax somewhat, but the monster doesn't vanish simply because we cover our eyes with our hands. If we try to turn a blind eye to stress, it can stay with us literally for years. A painkiller is not a cure.

If there *is* a magic bullet for stress, it is to become more self-aware. The simplest way to relieve physical tension is to notice it without our usual reaction of annoyance or fear. We don't have to 'do' anything. If we simply feel the tension with a degree of acceptance, it starts to loosen almost of its own accord.

Shall we do a simple exercise to illustrate this? Don't change your posture or put this book aside. Now slowly scan your body. You will probably find areas of excessive tension. These are parts of the body that are more tense than they need to be for the task of simply reading a book. Don't skip over them. Slow down and feel them. You may be twisted awkwardly in the chair, one shoulder may be held high, the jaw may be clenched or the breathing cramped. Try it out and see what you find!

Do you also see how tension releases, almost automatically, as soon as you notice it? The jaw drops a little, the shoulder softens, the head balances. It happens instinctively. We can enhance that effect by wriggling a little or 'breathing through' the tension. Notice how easy it is to relieve tension when you know exactly where it is and consider how long it would have remained otherwise. Of course, some discomfort may remain, but are you more relaxed than you were? The tension may well be 20 or 30 per cent less.

We never completely escape that slight residual discomfort that goes with having a living body. As a result, many people feel that partial relaxation is not worth it. They want all or nothing — distraction or oblivion. So, they choose to keep the engine running hot all day, and collapse at night. Unfortunately, falling asleep is not a magic cure for tension. If you are fairly relaxed when you go to bed, you slip easily into deep sleep. If you are tense, however, it may take several restless hours for your metabolic rate to sink to its lowest point.

When you sleep, tension doesn't just disappear. You are merely unconscious of it. Tension often remains in the body, relatively unchanged, waiting for you when you wake up. Many of us have muscles that have never relaxed in years.

Certainly, we never relax fully at night if we have been overly tense during the day. We dial the phone with a knot in our stomach. We sit hunched at our desks, unwilling to breathe. We read a book with clenched jaw and furrowed brow. This is excess tension. It is more than we need for the task at hand. It is also useless effort. We actually do the job less efficiently.

Yet we can release this strain as soon as we notice it. A student of mine, a dental technician, said, 'I do a hundred meditations a day.' She said she would find herself racing around the laboratory with her shoulders up around her ears. She would drop them. Two minutes later they were up again, and she would drop them again. 'I no longer have sore shoulders at the end of the day,' she said. All it takes is awareness.

The Physical Effects of Stress

Our response to a stressful situation often overshoots the mark. We may react to a snide comment, for example, as if we were being physically attacked. In fact, many of our ailments — hypertension, allergies, etc. — are our body's overreaction to an imagined threat. We are like certain Third World countries: we are more at risk from our own defence forces than the enemy outside.

Extreme or chronic stress galvanises the body for action. Adrenalin and thyroid hormones speed the metabolism. The heart beats faster, we breathe more rapidly. Sugar, insulin and cholesterol are released into the bloodstream. The digestive and immune systems shut down. Cortisol and endorphins, the body's painkillers, are released. The senses are heightened.

These inner chemicals prepare us for physical action. If we can act, they clear. If not, this inner fuel burns us. The most natural way to release it is to use the muscles of the body (not the head!). Our bodies are calling out to run, play squash, dig a garden or do aerobics ... or hit someone. The problem comes when we can't act physically.

After escaping a wild animal, our long-ago ancestors would wind down naturally. Most of *our* danger nowadays, however, is more obscure and chronic. We can't run from the boss, the alcoholic relative, the recession, or the hole in the ozone layer. The stress hormones gear us up for action, but what can we do, physically?

The fight-or-flight response is very healthy — in the short term. It is an energetic high and it often feels great — in the short term. When we can't put it into action and it stays for hours or even days, however, it poisons us. The fight-or-flight juices damage the arteries, cripple the immune system and predispose us to serious illness.

Some stress hormones are painkillers. They make our bodies numb. When under pressure, we treat our bodies like warhorses, whipping them into the battle. The more stressed we are, the less we feel our bodies. People in brawls typically don't feel their injuries until later, when they relax and the internal painkillers fade away. If you suspect you are suffering from stress, you can assume the damage is worse than you think.

When powering through the day, we hardly notice — and often ignore — the signs that the engine is overheating: headaches, indigestion, strain in the face. Eventually, the body shouts at us. For many, the first danger sign they acknowledge will be their last: a heart attack.

Why People Are Reluctant to Relax

Do you actually want to relax? This may seem a silly question, but there are many reasons why people are unwilling to relax.

Operating on high adrenalin has its pay-off, and we like it. We can become chemically addicted to stress. Cortisone and the endorphins are painkillers, like morphine, and adrenalin acts like an amphetamine. Stress is our own legal drug factory. We get a drug 'high', running on opiates and speed when stressed. It is like a bribe or reward that keeps us going when sanity would have us stop.

Alcoholics and drug addicts often feel powerful and in control of their destiny when they are high. Stress can give you the same effect. There is a pay-off for being Supermum, even if you feel shattered by bedtime.

Many people like to present a sparkling personality at work. It gives them drive and charm, and people like them. They need stress for their self-image in the same way that some body-builders need steroids. They use coffee and diet cola to keep themselves high. Their mask would crack if they came to work acting as tired as they actually felt.

Many people feel that unless they worry and run around a lot their world will fall apart: 'I'm so busy I haven't got a moment to relax!' There is no doubt that many people become high achievers precisely by operating on dangerously high stress levels. If you're thirty, you can manage it. If you are forty-two, you have to squeeze your adrenal glands hard or be overtaken by the youngsters.

'If I learn to meditate, will I lose my drive?' asked a 25-year-old insurance salesman. Although he was very successful, he chose to do what was good for him. He learnt to meditate and he did lose his passion for money. He left insurance and undertook arduous training as a yoga teacher and as a psychotherapist. He now has a successful practice, but he could have been a millionaire by now. Is that success or failure?

Staying tense or being habitually busy is an excellent way to avoid facing yourself. Tension blocks our deeper feelings. I remember a nun who walked out of one of my retreats. She was intelligent, articulate, a former headmistress and a writer. 'If I relax,' she said, 'negative emotions come up.' She found it too painful to see herself without her usual distractions.

Blocking feelings may be a good short-term strategy. For example, if you are under pressure during an illness or marriage break-up, it may not be useful to allow your feelings to emerge in force. You just need to hold yourself together and get through the experience. The stress hormones, after all, are like armour. They help you go into battle.

Conversely, you may feel awful and 'not yourself' if you relax deeply and withdraw from the inner drugs. Some people suffer what psychologists call 'relaxation-induced anxiety'. They hate the loss of control and can feel as if they are disintegrating if they relax.

The Process of Winding Down from Stress

Here we have a paradox. Relaxing is like convalescence: it is good for you, but often uncomfortable. If you had been involved in a car accident, for example, the stress hormones would have helped you cope. You walk away feeling good, or even 'high'. The after-effects of the shock, however, may be nausea, vomiting, weakness, shivering or an aching body, or any combination of these. You may be emotionally shaky for days. This is how nature balances your system after the extreme demands of the accident. You often feel bad before feeling good again.

If we are stressed, we have usually been abusing the body. When we notice this, we often get angry. We try to 'get rid of' the pain, as if it were a parasite. In reality, the pain is a part of us — our own flesh and blood.

To relax, it is best to be kind to ourselves. Relaxing the body should be like calming an upset child. It is best done with some love and patience. It you hit your child and tell it to 'stop whining', it won't calm down at all. All our bodies need is a little attention. If we accept that the pain is there, it often starts to move — in its own time and at its own pace. It doesn't help to be pushy.

We relax best if we don't fight the process. The body knows what to do. Our back or neck pain may seem like a huge, solid lump. It developed, however, through thousands of tiny moments of overreaction, and it won't disappear in a flash. Relaxation is the reverse process. It happens in thousands of tiny, stage-by-stage loosenings over time.

When we simply watch, wait and accept, the relaxation process can be very swift. People often come to a meditation class after work, stressed to the hilt. Their movements are rigid, their breathing is tight and they talk with animation to escape the emotional strain so obvious in their faces. Without meditation, they may still be revved up when they try to sleep, hours later.

In a class setting, however, they can relax to the edge of sleep in about six minutes, on average. I watch them as I guide them into meditation. At first, they sit rigidly in the chair — or fidget endlessly. Gradually, they make contact with their aches and pains. At a certain point, the body loosens with an involuntary sigh. Eventually the fine muscles of the face soften visibly. I know they have arrived. The process is under way.

SPOT MEDITATION: VISUAL OBJECT

This meditation can be practised during any free moment. You could be sitting at your desk, waiting at a bus stop or in your car. Often it is easier to give total attention to something for a minute than to try focusing for a longer time.

Instructions

- Pick out an interesting object in your field of vision. It could be a branch blowing in the wind, the pattern on someone's shirt, a shadow or a pot plant.
- Settle your mind there. Drop the inner talk. Shift into sensing.
- Let your eyes soften a little (i.e. don't stare). Use your eyes like a zoom lens. Let time slow down and explore the object at your leisure. Imagine its texture or smell, if appropriate. Allow associations to arise.
- Let your body soften and relax. Take a deep breath and sigh as you breathe out. Be aware of the object, your body and the stream of attention linking them. Tell other thoughts that arise to wait. You will attend to them shortly.
- Finally, let the object go, consciously. Check how your mind state has changed. Are you more calm and aware?

CHAPTER 4

How To Meditate —
The Core Instructions

This chapter is what you have been waiting for: a description of how to do a formal meditation. In particular, I will explain how to meditate on the breath. The breath will serve as our prototype for the other practices in this book.

The instructions for most meditations are the same: focus on the object and let other thoughts and sensations pass in the background. The main difference between meditations is the object upon which you choose to focus.

Ninety per cent of the effect of a meditation depends upon your depth of focus. The object itself is of secondary importance, but it does tend to set a mood. The breath meditation, for example, may have a different flavour to a mantra meditation or a visualisation.

A simple meditation such as the breath can have benefits that are not at all obvious at first. The breath is frequently the first meditation given to beginners, but it is also one of the most sophisticated of all practices. Over time, it develops in beautiful and unexpected ways. There are many reasons why more people meditate on the breath than on any other practice.

Why So Many People
Meditate on the Breath

The breath meditation seems to works well for about 60 per cent of meditators. It has all kinds of virtues:

1. It is a soothing thing upon which to meditate. The gentle ebb and flow of the breath caresses the body internally. It is soft, subtle, tactile and

reassuring. Perhaps it evokes memories of our time in the womb, when we were enveloped by our mother's breathing and heartbeat.

2. The breath is always with us. It is a very accessible meditation. Any time, any place, we can drop into a few moments of breath meditation.

3. The breath changes as we relax. It exactly mirrors our degree of emotional tension or relaxation. When tense, the breath feels constricted and is held in the upper chest. As we loosen up, the breath drops through the body. Eventually the breath becomes delicate, soft and spacious. By watching the changing breath, we also notice the whole body relaxing and the mind detaching from thought.

4. The deeper we relax, the more evasive the breath becomes. It becomes very light and often stops for seconds at a time. This forces us to be more attentive as we relax — which is never easy to do. We also get a taste of timelessness and space in the gap between out-breath and in-breath.

5. The breath mixes well with other meditation objects. It is transparent. People often focus on the breath while also saying a mantra or affirmation, or while watching thoughts or scanning the body. It is a good template on which to build a more complex meditation.

6. The breath stimulates memory and dream imagery. It is like a screen, or crystal ball, on which our entire life eventually passes before our eyes. This inner vision seems to occur more frequently with the breath than with other meditations.

7. Finally, the breath leads to a deep self-awareness. It is no mistake that the word *breath* in both English and Sanskrit is related to words like 'psyche', 'soul' and 'life force'. The breath can take us to those inner spaces.

Instructions for the Breath Meditation

Most of these instructions could apply to any meditation. Only sections 3 and 4 specifically relate to the breath. You can regard the following instructions as a template for any other formal meditation.

1. PREPARATION

Choose a relatively quiet place and allow yourself fifteen minutes in which you will not be interrupted. If you need to, have soft music playing in the background. Find a comfortable position that allows you to breathe easily. For most people, a straight-backed padded chair is ideal.

2. SHIFT FROM THINKING TO SENSING

Let thoughts go. Be aware of the sounds around you. Take a deep breath or two and sigh. Notice how you are sitting. Scan the body, releasing any unnecessary tension.

3. FOCUS ON THE BREATH

Go to some place where you can feel the breath easily. It could be in the belly, the chest, the throat or the nostrils. Enjoy the ebb and flow. Feel the body expand and contract. Stay with the breath while tolerating the other thoughts and sensations that inevitably arise. Return to the breath whenever you lose it.

4. COUNT THE BREATHS

To stay on track, count the breaths up to five or ten repeatedly. Say the count on the out-breath, and the word 'and' on the in-breath. For example, 'one ... and two ... and three ...', and so on.

5. NOTICE THE SIGNS OF THE BODY RELAXING

After a few minutes, notice how the body changes. Feel the body becoming heavy. Notice tingling or warmth on the skin. Let the aches and pains, or the tiredness within you, come to the surface. Feel the breath becoming lighter and more gentle.

6. NAME THE DISTRACTIONS

If you are persistently distracted by something, you can 'name' the content of that thought or sensation. This acknowledges it, but also distances you from it. Return to the breath.

7. EMERGE SLOWLY

Have your eyes open for the last minute of the meditation. Just rest quietly. You don't need to start thinking just because your eyes are open. Stay in the present moment, aware of sight, sounds or body sensations. Notice the effect of the meditation. Is the body more relaxed and the mind slower than when you started?

Let me now explain some of the above instructions in more detail.

Shift from Thinking to Sensing

This usually means noticing the sights, sounds and body sensations of the moment. When you are fully present, you are free of thought — especially thoughts of the past and future. Don't worry if some sensations are not to your liking — if there's too much noise, for example, or your body hurts. The stimuli don't have to be pleasant. Sensing alone is enough to slow down the mind.

The body relaxes gradually. For the first minute or two, we tend to shuffle a little, becoming aware of tensions and loosening them up. It is useful to do this deliberately, by scanning the body up or down, unlocking each part in turn.

Don't over-control the body. People often feel they must hold the body perfectly still in order to relax. Relaxing, however, slows your metabolic rate and shifts the body towards sleep. We don't control the body while asleep. Similarly, we don't over--control the body while meditating. Good meditators often move slightly as they meditate. Consciously or not, they make subtle shifts as the minutes go by. The face and shoulders soften, the breathing becomes more fluid and small postural adjustments occur. As the body loses its rigidity, it may rock very slightly under the influence of the heartbeat.

Focus on the Breath

Focusing means 'bringing the object into focus', rather like adjusting a camera lens. You are focusing well when you see detail you didn't notice at first. You feel the luxurious movement through the body. You notice exactly where and when the breath stops and starts.

Ideally, you become intimate with the breath. You enjoy it. You feel it caressing you. You can use the breath to massage the tensions within you. Focusing is easy if you have interest, or can cultivate an interest, in the object. (Many people focus on their object in very cursory fashion. They count the breaths mechanically, while also thinking about work and what they will have for tea that night ... Then they wonder why their meditation seems mediocre.)

Only rarely can you focus so deeply that other thoughts and sensations disappear. The mind naturally goes in and out. It oscillates from the breath to other thoughts and sensations and back again. Don't be annoyed by this. It is the natural rhythm of the mind.

If your day has been demanding, you may spend more time out than in. You usually focus well only when you have 'ticked off' the other preoccupations. If these are many, this will take a long time. Be patient. In meditation, you don't aim to get rid of thoughts. It is quite enough to watch them with detachment.

Counting the Breaths

In most meditations, the mind is quite passive. Since it can become too passive and fall asleep, you give it a simple, repetitive task to keep it awake. In this case, you count the breaths.

Counting breaths is easy at first. As you relax, however, you often lose the count. Counting is a warning device. When you can't remember what the next number is, the alarm bells go off. You are obviously drifting. When you find you are lost, don't be annoyed. Just drop the thought and return to the counting.

There are several ways to count. Some people just count on the out-breath. They say 'one' as they breath out, 'two' on the next out-breath, and so on. Some people double-count. They say 'one' on the in-breath and 'one' on the out-breath, and so on. I suggest people use the word 'and' on the in-breath, and say the count on the out-breath: 'One ... and ... two ... and ... three ...'.

People usually count up to five or ten breaths at a time, and then start again at the number one. Musicians may prefer to count in multiples of four. You may not like counting at all. I once had five accountants in a class. Counting was not their idea of relaxing. You could just say 'in … out …' as you breathe.

Counting the breaths is not essential. It is quite enough just to feel each breath. If you are well focused on the breath, you don't need to count.

By counting, you don't try to control the breaths. This is not the time to try breathing 'properly' or to do formal yogic breathing exercises. We are using the breath just as a prop upon which to hang the mind. If we try to breathe deeply and regularly, we may prevent it going through its natural changes and so over-oxygenate the body. This can make you a little jumpy or faint, rather than help you relax.

Nonetheless, many people can't focus on the breath without trying to control it. This is not a problem, so long as they control it as little as possible. It is quite okay to make the breathing a little smoother and to round off the edges. It may even help you focus better.

Notice the Signs of the Body Relaxing

The body chemistry changes as we relax. It is very useful to notice this, regardless of the kind of meditation you are doing.

First, noticing the body holds your attention and keeps you alert. It keeps you in the present and in the sense world. Secondly, it affirms that you are on the right track. The meditation is working. Thirdly, you eventually notice how individual thoughts and feelings immediately resonate in your body. You see how one thought makes you tense, and another makes you relax. You understand the body–mind connection directly.

I describe the signs of relaxation more fully in the next chapter.

Name the Distractions

When you focus on the breath, you are inevitably aware of other things. Most of these are not distractions. You notice them, but they don't necessarily take you away from the breath. It is quite okay to notice the noise of traffic or a door slamming, or to be aware of back pain or a headache. These are all sensations of the present moment, and don't necessarily distract you.

Some things, however, usually thoughts of past and future, are real distractions. They suck you away from the breath, they hang around, they won't let you go. So what can you do about them?

First, you try to ignore them. You turn your back on them and look deeper into the breath. After five or ten seconds, the thought often dissolves of its own accord. It is worth remembering that we actually ignore the vast majority of our thoughts most of the time. Only a few are strong enough to demand our attention.

Trying to ignore or 'block out' or 'switch off' emotionally charged thoughts is, however, a crude strategy. It rarely works all the time or for all thoughts, and often doesn't work at all. It often makes you more irritable, as yet another unwanted visitor knocks at the door.

Some distractions are too big and too obvious to be ignored. In this case, we use another strategy. We 'name' the distraction. We acknowledge its presence, but don't react to it. We ask what the distraction is and name the content of the thought: 'Food ... television ... money ... Susan ...'.

Distractions usually grab us from behind. We find we have been thinking about Susan for two minutes before we realise it. By saying 'Susan', however, we pull free from the thought and see it from a distance. This gives us a choice we didn't have before: we can continue thinking or return to the breath.

Naming the distraction serves to 'pigeonhole' it. Susan, and the tangle of thoughts around her, does not disappear. We simply hold her at arm's length and put her on the shelf. She still has a place in the mind, but at the periphery. Although we know she is present, we can still focus on the breath.

Don't try to name everything — just the big ones. And don't name at all if you can just let thoughts pass regardless. Naming the distractions is not a technique for everyone. Use it only if it works for you.

You can use general, or precise, words when you name. You could, for example, simply say 'distraction', or you could say 'past' or 'future' if your thought is about one or the other. You could name the content of the thought: 'work' or 'David' or 'food'. You could name the emotion or mind state: 'sleepy' or 'restless' or 'irritated' or 'bored'. You could also name things that are part of the present moment if they are disturbing you. You could say 'headache' or 'garbage truck' or 'heartbeat' or 'itchy nose'.

By focusing deeply, you try to escape the distractions. Naming, however, is a more tolerant and accommodating approach. Instead of trying to purge your unwanted thoughts, you negotiate a peace with them. It is like saying to a thought 'I know you're there, but I'm busy just now. Can you wait?'

What If You Don't Like To Meditate on the Breath?

Of course, you don't have to focus on the breath. There are many other possibilities. You may wonder what the best kind of meditation is. Is it an ancient Hindu mantra? Or a Tibetan or New Age visualisation? Or something more simple, like the breath? Perhaps you should use something that has been devised 'especially for the Western mind'.

Groups like to claim their meditations are better, or more modern, or more ancient or more powerful than the rest. Most of this, however, is packaging and advertising. Whether your meditation is good or mediocre depends not on the object, but on your depth of focus. To put it another way, it is better to meditate on your big toe than on a pretty visualisation if your big toe holds your attention better.

There are many 'one-size-fits-all' groups that claim their practice is better than all the rest. People, however, have different temperaments. There is no one practice that suits everyone. Although mantra, for example, is an excellent practice, I find it suits only about a third of all people who come to learn meditation. If you join a group that only uses a mantra and mantra don't suit you, you may feel like a failure when, in fact, you are simply working with the wrong technique.

A meditation, like a medicine, is not good or bad in itself. It has to suit the person. Even penicillin can be a poison to someone who is allergic to it. It is good to try out different techniques and see what feels right.

This is not hard to do. It should be like tasting new food at a restaurant. If it looks and smells good, you eat it. It doesn't have to be perfect. In time, you will change it to suit yourself anyway.

I like to offer people a smorgasbord of practices. You can meditate on the breath or the body, on mantra or affirmations, on sounds, visual objects, visualisations or combinations of the above. People usually find their preferences quickly. They also find that certain practices — such as mantra, for example — are good if they are sleepy; and other practices — such as the breath — are better when they are more awake.

Some practices have secondary effects that are not always obvious. The breath meditation is generally soothing and takes you inwards. Scanning the body raises more self-awareness, but can be less relaxing. Listening to sounds induces a sense of space and light and takes you out of yourself. Meditating on visual objects enhances your sense of beauty and connects you with the world around you. Mantra and affirmations commonly have a hypnotic effect, and so on.

These differences will become clear in later chapters.

CHAPTER 5

What Happens
When You Relax?

Stress, like pain, can be a good friend. It tells us when our way of living is dangerous to our health. We usually don't want to hear this message, so we try to ignore it. This almost seems to work, except that the messenger makes quite a noise battering on the door. So, not surprisingly, we often fail to notice the signs of stress.

Strange to say, we also misread the signs of relaxation. This is because we lose awareness as we relax. The mind drifts amid thoughts and fantasies. We 'space out' a little and can't say what it is we are thinking about and, eventually, we fall asleep. During this process, the mind is not particularly conscious. So, we don't notice what relaxation feels like because we are not 'there' when it happens.

Consequently, we don't know what it is we are aiming for. Oblivion, or the absence of pain, is a rather evasive target. Relaxation, on the other hand, is much more positive. If we know exactly what it feels like and how the process unfolds, we can get there fast.

I start my courses by guiding people into a state of rest. Years ago, I would do this with people lying on the floor. I soon found they did better in chairs—they stayed awake! Even in chairs, people gradually slip into a state I call 'body asleep, mind awake'. The body may literally go to sleep, but the mind is awake enough to know what is happening. I ask, again and again throughout the session, 'What is happening? What does it feel like to be relaxed?' In this way, the participants start to recognise their personal landmarks. After the session, we discuss what people noticed. It is often not what they expected. Although we all relax at least once a day when we fall asleep, it is still unknown territory to most of us.

The notion of staying alert while we relax may seem paradoxical. People would prefer just to let go and allow themselves to relax. Unfortunately, this approach rarely works. An uncontrolled mind doesn't relax quickly or well. It wanders. It goes back into thoughts and worries. Eventually it falls asleep, trailing remnants of unfinished thoughts behind it. If we stay awake, however, we can pick ourselves free of thoughts and steer ourselves down rapidly. It helps to keep the hands on the steering wheel and to have the headlights on.

Going to the 'body asleep, mind awake' state is just the first stage. Eventually one can be awake while dreaming (still sitting up in a chair) and awake in the dreamless sleep state (in which all thoughts and sensations vanish). Staying awake as the body descends into deep sleep leads into the trance states of the Indian yogis.

Recognising the Signs of Relaxation

The central nervous system operates like a thermostat. The sympathetic branch of the nervous system winds us up. This is when we are mentally or physically active. It raises the level of tension in the body and our metabolic rate (the rate at which we burn energy). At a certain point, the process peaks and the reverse occurs. The parasympathetic branch of the nervous system starts to wind us down. This is when we are relaxing, being less active and conserving energy. Our metabolic rate drops.

By meditating, we consciously switch on the parasympathetic nervous system and lower the metabolic rate. As we relax, the body physiology changes. If we relax quickly, it changes dramatically. Many observable changes occur, but most people will notice the following: the body feeling heavy or light, tingling on the skin, aches and pains emerging, and the breath becoming lighter.

These are the four main signs of relaxation for which I ask my students to look. Some notice them immediately. Others rarely notice them at all. Some people are very sensitive to their bodies, while others live more in their heads or feelings. If you do notice these signs, however, they reassure you that you are relaxing well.

They also act as a biofeedback loop. In other words, simply noticing them takes you deeper.

HEAVINESS OR LIGHTNESS

'My body felt like lead.'

'My hands felt like they were fused together.'

'I felt I was sinking deeper and deeper into myself.'

'I felt heavy, just also as if I was floating.'

'I couldn't feel my hands [arms, legs, body]. I wiggled my fingers to make sure they were still there.'

'My body felt huge.'

Adrenalin 'lifts' the body. It provides a restless chemical charge to all the muscles of the body that keeps them on edge, ready for action. As we stop secreting adrenalin (because we are relaxing), the charge fades. The muscles seem to sag. The body surrenders to the floor or chair. Arms, legs, the head or the whole body feel heavy, numb or still. When you notice sensations like this, you know you have switched on the parasympathetic nervous system.

Usually, we are always moving slightly. Most people don't sit still for more than ten seconds at a time. This movement activates nerve spindles in the muscles that send messages to the brain such as 'the elbow has moved half an inch to the left', and so on. As the restlessness fades, however, the body becomes quite still and those signals aren't triggered. The brain can interpret this as the body feeling numb or floating, or disconnected. People lose contact with their hands or feet, or feel very little below the neck.

For brief moments, we may seem to lose the body completely. This is when we are just at the edge of sleep, but still awake enough to enjoy it. All thoughts of the day have vanished, and we are about to drop into oblivion. If we watch ourselves, we see that the body tends to relax in the following sequence, with some stages overlapping: heavy, numb, still, light or floating, disconnected, vanishing.

These sensations are actually quite easy to notice if you stay alert and look for them.

TINGLING OR WARMTH ON THE SKIN

'My skin felt warm and tingly (or itchy).'
'I felt pleasantly warm all over.'
'My hands and feet became quite hot.'
'I could feel the pulse in my hands [neck, face …].'

When we are tense, the blood drains from the skin to the large inner muscles in preparation for fight-or-flight. The reverse happens when we relax. The blood thins out and flows back to the skin, making it warm and tingly, especially in the hands and face. Meditation immediately improves your circulation.

The skin comes alive and seems to tingle slightly. It is like when we get out of a shower or finish some aerobic exercise or have a shot of alcohol. This sensation is quite subtle, but most people can detect it if they look for it. For some people, the flow of blood is very obvious. Their hands get puffy and wedding rings feel tight. People who suffer cold hands and feet are often pleasantly surprised by the flow of warmth. One student told me he has to take off his shoes when he meditates because his feet get so hot.

The increased blood flow also loosens up congested muscles. These may feel less rigid, or more soft and pliable. Some meditators actually feel the blood moving in surges, like waves upon the shore. Usually about half the class can feel the pulsing of the blood.

ACHES AND PAINS SURFACING

'I didn't realise how tense I was.'
'I thought I was fine when I came in here. Then I noticed this awful headache and my stomach is sore, too.'
'It took a long time for the pain in my shoulders to go.'
'I was more tired than I thought.'

When tense, we secrete adrenalin and cortisol, which are natural analgesics. When we relax, these hormonal painkillers fade away and the little aches and pains in the body become obvious. Our latent tiredness often comes to the surface when we give it the chance. We may find sore spots emerging everywhere — eyes, neck, shoulders, head, stomach.

Pain is often part of relaxing. For example, you may sit down after working for a couple of hours in the garden. The energy is still running through you and you feel great. Five minutes later, however, as you relax, you realise you are aching all over.

This can annoy people who see relaxing as a kind of oblivion. They often don't want to be so aware of their aches and pains. Yet their arrival is actually a good sign that a person started to relax. I encourage my students to welcome these aches and pains. If we fight pain, it stays. If we accept pain, it finds its own way out of the body. Pain that is obviously releasing can, in fact, be pleasant. It is like the 'good' pain you experience during a massage, when the masseur's fingers loosen up the sore spots.

A common sequence is 'no pain, more pain, less pain'. First, the students feel no pain because they are still tense. As they relax, their discomforts surface and may be worse than they expected. By the end of the meditation, however, the headache is fading and the shoulders feel better. The tension continues to release after the meditation is over.

CHANGES IN THE BREATHING

'My breathing became very light, and often stopped for long periods.'
'My breathing went right down into my belly.'
'My breathing was quite erratic. Sometimes I had to take a deep breath.'
'I felt I wasn't breathing deeply enough.'

Our breathing reflects our level of tension. As we relax, our breathing mirrors that process. The breathing commonly passes through the following stages as we meditate. Initially, it is tense, then it becomes deep, then light and occasionally stops altogether.

If we are tense, the breath feels short and tight. We tend to breathe from the upper chest only and hold the breath. This gives us a certain energy charge in case we have to respond quickly to something.

As we relax, we gradually let the out-breath go. This doesn't happen instantly. The shift from tense, upper-body breathing to loose, open breathing often occurs in jerky stages over two or three minutes. The belly eventually loosens up and we now seem to be breathing deeply.

Finally, the breathing can become very light. As our metabolic rate slows down, and our minds become quiet, we don't need much air. We breathe, after all, for a reason. We need oxygen to burn energy in the cells to maintain the level of activity in the body and mind. Tight shoulders burn up a lot of energy. When the shoulders, and other tight muscles, let go, we need much less energy. And so we breathe less.

If the mind also becomes very still, when we breathe out, there can often be a long pause before the new in-breath. This can be very lovely. The breath dissolves into space. It is a moment outside of time, when everything within us seems to stop. The breathing now feels light, delicate and spacious.

OTHER SIGNS OF RELAXATION

The digestive system shuts down when we are tense and comes to life when we relax. Some people start to salivate and have to swallow now and then. 'I know I am relaxed when I have to swallow,' said one student. Other people have gurgling stomachs.

Occasionally, people feel a little nauseous. A tense stomach is often numb. As we relax, more blood and sensation flow into the area. If you have been tense for several hours, the first sensations you notice may be uncomfortable ones. Old Buddhist texts describe nausea as a sign of relaxation. I call it 'meditator's nausea' because it usually stops when the meditation is over.

We become more fluid as we relax. Gastric juices flow. Blood circulation increases. For no apparent reason, the eyes may start to water.

Other signs of relaxation are more subjective and personal. Some people become more aware of their underlying emotional state. A few see colours, when the words fade away. At the edge of sleep, some people see fleeting dream images. Some feel a sense of great space, or lightness. Others feel centred, peaceful and at home in themselves. It is good to know your personal landmarks.

Know You Are Doing It Right

People often wonder if they are meditating correctly. They are often seeking some ideal state — and they are not sure if they have arrived or not. For any meditator, however, the basic skill is to be able to relax quickly and consciously. In other words, you need to be able to turn on the parasympathetic nervous system at will.

The meditator can check if the signs of relaxation are present. Does the body feel heavy, or numb or light? Is there a gentle warmth or tingling on the skin? Does the breathing feel soft and delicate? Does the meditator feel more in touch with his or her body, and its aches and pains? Does the body feel close to sleep? If these signs are there, a person knows he or she is on the right track.

When you are tense, your body feels solid. As you relax, it feels more fluid. As you approach the 'body asleep, mind awake' state, it feels spacious, almost dissolving into air or the inner darkness.

It is good to realise that a relaxed state is not automatically pain-free or happy. Meditation relaxes you, but it is not necessarily a 'happy' pill. You can't solve all the problems in your life in one meditation. The mind may still be upset, although the body is relaxed.

Even if you are not perfectly happy, it is healthy to be relaxed. When we relax, the inner juices flow. The medical evidence says that meditation releases muscular tension, increases circulation, lowers high blood pressure, and so on. With practice, you actually feel these, and many other changes, within you. You now meditate with confidence. You can feel it working.

Some people are apprehensive at the first class. 'I've always been uptight. My doctor told me to come here, but I don't think I'll ever relax.' Yet after two or three weeks, they know the feeling in their own flesh and blood, and they can bring it about at will.

SPOT MEDITATION: RANDOM SOUNDS

We are always surrounded by sound, which we usually ignore. In this meditation, you actively listen to sound — the distant traffic, the air-conditioning, a bird call, your own breathing, the wind in the roof. It may not seem very interesting, perhaps, but notice what happens. When you listen carefully, the past and future disappear. For a moment at least, there is just you and the sound and not a thought in sight.

When focusing on random sounds, it is very hard to think of other things. If you do, you lose the next sound. Their very randomness keeps us on our toes. We don't know from where the next sound will come. In order to listen well, we can't think — and the very listening keeps us alert.

Many meditations make us introspective and withdrawn. Random sounds, however, take us outside ourselves. They give us a sense of space. Our mind spreads hundreds of yards in all directions. We realise we can relax while still in touch with the outer world.

Often there are gaps between sounds. If we can rest there with nothing to focus on, waiting for the next sound, we get a taste for complete silence and the vastness of space that surrounds us all.

You can do this meditation anywhere, inside or out, alone or in public. Since you don't have to close your eyes or change your posture, you can meditate without the people around you realising. You may sit in a meeting, looking intelligent and thoughtful. In fact, you've put the mind on hold and are just waiting for the next sound.

Instructions

- Take a deep breath or two and let the body settle.
- Open up your mind. Let sounds come in from all directions. Notice their variety. Notice the little background sounds to which you would normally never pay attention.
- Get interested in sounds. Try to catch them the moment they arise. Follow them to the very end. Feel their texture and colour, and notice them overlap.
- Don't strive after sounds. Open up the mind and wait. Let the sounds come to you. If there are gaps, then enjoy them. If the mind drifts back to thought, come back to the next sound, whatever it is.
- Keep a background awareness of your body. Make sure you are not holding your breath. Feel the body relaxing. If you want, imagine the sounds resonating through your body.

CHAPTER 6

Sitting Comfortably and Breathing Naturally

Being Comfortable, Balanced and Alert

Whenever I mention the word 'posture' in class, at least one person shuffles guiltily and attempts to 'sit up straight'. Posture is important in meditation, but it is much misunderstood. Many people never attempt to meditate, for example, because they feel they have to sit cross-legged on the floor.

What matters is not the posture we take, but how we hold ourselves in it. In fact, we can meditate in any posture. We can meditate sitting in a chair or on the floor. Or walking, fast or slow. Or lying down, on our side or on our back. Or standing. Or in any posture in between. These are all traditional postures in the East.

There are, however, guidelines. Your posture should be comfortable (but not super-comfortable), balanced and open (so your breathing is not constricted), and alert. You can't expect to meditate well slumped in an easy chair, for example, or curled up in bed. The most important general rule is: don't slump.

The simplest way to relax is to notice the moment-to-moment sensations of tension and relaxation in your body. Does your body feel tight, hard and locked-up? Or is it soft, loose and open? Asking yourself this is to be aware of posture. Tension usually releases if you are aware of it. Good posture 'grows from within' as you become more attuned to yourself.

'Having eaten and rested, the wanderer goes to a wild place and sits comfortably at the foot of a tree ...' These instructions are 2500 years old.

They come from the Buddha, and emphasise the need to be comfortable. There is enough discomfort in the mind without stressing the body as well.

It may seem obvious that you need to be comfortable if you want to relax. Yet many Westerners go through misery for years trying to sit cross-legged. Do they feel it must be better if it hurts? They may assume that any 'spiritual' discipline necessarily involves mastering the demands of the flesh, and that to be comfortable is almost a weakness. These ideas are often not conscious, but they are all the stronger for being deeply engraved in our Western consciousness.

Meditation attempts to integrate body and mind. The East has a profound respect for the wisdom of the body, which is reflected in the spiritual disciplines of yoga and the martial arts. I analysed a dream recently in which a woman dreamt that peasants from her home country were inviting her into the wheat fields to listen to the sound of the earth. Finding good posture should be like this. If you listen to your body, it will tell you what it wants.

Using a Chair

Most Westerners find that a straight-backed, padded office chair is ideal. It should be low enough for you to have both feet firmly on the ground. If you are short, you may find your feet dangle. In this case, prop up your feet with cushions so you feel more stable.

Even better, cut the legs of the chair to the right size. Most chairs are designed for the average-sized man and are too high for many women. I had 5 centimetres cut off all the chair legs at the meditation centre. It is worth doing if you plan to do a lot of meditating.

Some people like armrests, some don't. Armrests can prevent the shoulders slumping and give you a feeling of security. They are good for the elderly and infirm, or for you, at any age, if you happen to feel 'elderly and infirm'.

When sitting in a chair, the right-angle between torso and legs can block the breathing a little. This can be overcome somewhat by spreading the legs apart and letting the belly hang out. It also creates a stable tripod effect with your two legs and your bottom. This is the 'samurai' posture. It does not look very feminine, but it supports your back well.

Sitting on the Floor

Sitting on the floor is excellent if you are relatively supple and strong. Since most people don't sit well on the floor, however, let me first describe how not to do it.

Most people, when they are sitting on the floor, start with good posture. Very soon, however, their shoulders slump and their chest collapses. This blocks their breathing, creates pain in the back and induces a physiological depression in the body. You can try it out right now. Let your shoulder slump and notice how your mood changes.

Slumping shoulders induce a blocked, low-energy state, which inhibits the vitality of the body. You often feel a mild depression as well, a kind of 'leave-me-alone' mood. It is like lying in bed half-asleep when you don't want to rise and face the day. People who meditate a lot, especially in religious groups, may fall into this trap. They can shut down their bodies and minds, but their posture reinforces a slightly depressed, escapist state of mind.

To sit well on the floor, you need BIG cushions. You need to get the hips well up above the knees. Otherwise, it is almost impossible not to slump. Zen practitioners are good models to follow. They use big round cushions, at least 20 centimetres deep and solidly padded.

The cushions can be so large that they tilt slightly as you sit on the edge of them. Some people, like myself, place a smaller cushion or a rolled-up blanket underneath the cushion at the back to increase the tilt. This throws the hips forward, supports the lower back well and opens the front of the body so you breathe easily. The effect is similar to that produced by an ergonomic kneeling chair.

If you sit against a wall, or the end of a bed, it helps to have a small cushion in the small of your back to prevent slumping.

Many people meditate on kneeling stools. These are easy to construct. They are usually just a long narrow plank about 60 centimetres long by 15 centimetres wide. Legs at each end hold it up about 20 centimetres off the ground. The seat is usually tilted forward about 30 degrees, to open up the hips. Your legs go underneath in kneeling posture. These stools are very comfortable. Many people who feel under pressure to meditate on the floor finish up with them, after trying for years to sit cross-legged.

Reclining Chairs and Lying Down

Reclining chairs are excellent if you are very tense, or have a bad back or neck, or are exhausted. In such circumstances, if you sit up, you may be too uncomfortable to relax adequately. Nonetheless, people who use reclining chairs often have rather vague meditations.

Posture gives a message to the mind. To lie down, for most of us, is to say 'go to sleep'. If we can overcome this conditioning and stay alert, lying down is a good posture.

Sleep, however, is very alluring. I often meet long-time meditators who complain they have trouble with sleepiness. Since they can obviously relax, I suggest they change their posture. They could try sitting up, for example, or keeping their eyes open. My suggestions, however, often fall on deaf ears. 'I couldn't possible relax like that,' they say — and go off to sleep again.

Of course, some people meditate in order to go to sleep. They can feel a little shamefaced about this, but a good night's sleep is worth having. Generally, if you sit up to meditate, you stay alert. If you do exactly the same meditation lying down, you fall asleep. Just changing the posture changes the effect. So long as you don't always meditate lying down, it is fine to meditate to put yourself to sleep.

Good posture grows from within, over time. The posture of good meditators usually becomes more elegant and balanced as the minutes pass. In contrast, beginners often slump as the meditation progresses. It shows that they are not very awake. They are relaxing, but not meditating very well.

Breathing and the Issue of Control

Good posture opens the body and gives the breath, and other body juices, room to move. Yet when we sense the breathing, we find it rarely flows with perfect ease. There may be subtle blockages everywhere. These tend to loosen as we notice them. We can improve our posture just by watching the flow of the breath and other sensations within us.

Can you watch the breath without controlling it? Relaxed breathing is often erratic — now shallow, now deep, occasionally stopping. This is quite natural, but many people are disconcerted by the natural activity of their bodies. They wonder if they are breathing correctly or breathing enough.

Some people want to control the breath to 'make it better.' Some even feel they should control their heartbeat, too. We may not realise how much we fear and try to dominate our bodies. This habit builds up over decades. Some people hold themselves very tight; others are more trusting. One person learns meditation because 'I want to make myself relax'; others 'let themselves' relax. The latter usually do better.

So what is relaxed breathing? Notice your breath when you are almost asleep or look at a sleeping baby. The breath is unlikely to be perfectly regular. The whole body expands and contracts. There may be the odd, deep sigh and times when breathing is short, or stops altogether. The inner feeling is one of timeless space and uncontrolled movement without boundaries. This is relaxed breathing. It is can be quite different from what we actually think of as 'good' breathing.

As an infant grows, it learns to inhibit the flow of life within. Certain emotions are too overwhelming or socially unacceptable to be allowed to surface. The simplest way to suppress them is to lock up the breathing, which then becomes habitually jerky, stiff and nervous. Much of our physical tension comes from the continual struggle to suppress unwanted feeling.

Meditation should be a gradual loosening of unnecessary control. This can be quite difficult. The entrenched bureaucrats of former communist states want to stay in control. Our nervous systems do, too. If chronic anxiety and hard work have 'got you where you are today', you are naturally reluctant to give it up. Your doctor may tell you to relax, but your conditioning says 'No! Hang on!'

Many people try to relax by controlling the whole process. They try to find the correct way to breathe. They may experiment with yogic deep breathing or control the breath with counting exercises, or they may try to make their breathing smooth and regular.

Two or three deep breaths, or a minute or two of yogic breathing, to start a meditation is good. These concentration exercises settle the mind, but are still control mechanisms. It is important to go a step further and let the breathing be free. We still need discipline, but only to dismantle the rigidity that blocks the natural breath.

Of course, many people can't focus on the breath without trying to control it. This is just their nature. It is not a problem as long as they control it as little as possible. Relaxing should be like sleep: we don't control our breathing when we sleep, nor do we need to control it as we relax. Meditation controls the mind so the body can be free.

Control is not automatically 'bad' and freedom 'good'. We need a little of both. Westerners, however, usually err on the side of control. Christianity emphasises the human race's dominion over nature. Although we may no longer be outwardly Christian, that attitude can still cast its shadow over us as we sit down to meditate. We often feel we should impose our will on the breath and the body. We are unwilling to trust it.

The Eastern assumptions are different. They assume that nature can be trusted. The breath and the body are wise. Unlike our personal egos, they have been around for millions of years. The body knows how to breathe. It knows exactly what to do, for inner health and balance, if we give it half a chance. We just have to get our interfering mind out of the way. We don't need to impose good posture or a beautiful state of mind on ourselves. They grow from within if we listen to ourselves. We start at the most basic level: watching our posture and breathing.

MEDITATION: BODY SCAN

In any meditation, it helps to have something systematic to do. Here, we scan the body in deliberate stages, from top to bottom, or bottom to top. Body scanning is a meditation on posture and breathing. It is an excellent practice in its own right and it can be used as a preliminary to other techniques.

This practice extends the 'countdown' meditation of chapter 2 (see page 22). We divide the body into the same seven regions and deliberately shift from one to the next — but we do it slowly. We give ourselves more time to explore the sensations in each place. These could be tingling, heat, tension, pain, pressure, the pulse — in fact, anything at all.

Obviously, body scanning is similar to the breath meditation. In body scanning, you focus on the body sensations while having a

MEDITATION: BODY SCAN (continued)

background awareness of the breath. In the breath meditation, you do the reverse. There are also other important differences, which is why people generally prefer one or the other.

The mind is more active when you scan. This suits people with active minds. It keeps them occupied. There is much to see and do and feel, so you are not so readily distracted. The breath meditation is more tranquil. The mind ideally stays in one place. It has a peripheral, but not detailed, awareness of the body. The body relaxes mainly because the mind settles. This suits people who prefer simplicity and stillness.

Body scanning is systematic. You follow on from one place to the next. You become aware of subtle tensions, and that helps them free up. Body scanning, in other words, is engrossing and systematically unravels the tension in the body.

Body scanning gives you a lot upon which to focus. Nonetheless, the mind will still want to think of other things. When it does this, just 'name the distractions' and give them space at the edges of the mind.

Instructions

Sit comfortably and shake your body loose. Survey your body and release any obvious tension. Take a couple of deep breaths and let go completely as you breathe out.

Scan the body at your own speed, while counting the breaths. Become interested in the subtle detail. Don't try to fix things up or make yourself relax. Just watching is enough. You could spend one or five or even ten breaths in each of the following regions:

1. Scalp and forehead (notice tingling, pulsing, pressure ...)
2. The face and lower part of the head (soften the eyes, let the mouth and jaw go slack)
3. Neck, throat, shoulders, arms and hands (like stroking or massaging the body with your mind)
4. Chest and upper back (feel the lungs expand and contract)

MEDITATION: BODY SCAN (continued)

5. Diaphragm and solar plexus (feel the movement of the lower ribs)
6. The belly and lower back (feel the soft organs move slightly as you breathe)
7. Hips, legs and feet (feel or imagine the breath dropping through your body)

Now focus on the breath anywhere in the body. Count the breaths. Be aware of the background sensations of relaxation: heaviness, tingling, aches and pains. 'Tick off' the distractions as they arise by naming them.

Stay with the breath as long as you like, or scan again. Scanning down is relaxing in effect. Scanning upwards raises energy and keep you more alert.

Variations

There are many different body-scanning practices. They go by names such as progressive muscle relaxation, Yoga Nidra, Kundalini, 'opening the chakras', and so on. In some way, they all focus on the subtle play of life, or sensation or 'energy', in the body. Since these mirror the activity of the mind, they can be very rewarding to watch.

The meditation given, however, is an excellent starting point, and there are several ways you can augment it.

1. WHITE LIGHT MEDITATION Imagine light, water, nectar or pure consciousness flowing through the body from top to bottom (see pages 96–97 for more details).

2. BREATHING THROUGH THE BODY Imagine you are 'breathing through', or caressing, each part of the body in turn. Comb out the tensions as you go. Or imagine you are massaging each part of the body with your mind.

3. CHAKRAS Let the mind rest in the central point of each of the seven regions. Stay there until it feels loose and open, and then move on to the next centre. If you want, you can say an affirmation or mantra or visualisation while doing so.

CHAPTER 7

Awareness — The Art of Detachment

Detachment Is the Fruit of Meditation

Meditation is one-pointed focus. This is an ancient Indian definition of meditation, but who wants to just watch the breath, or say a mantra, for the rest of their lives? No one. That would be boring beyond belief. The breath is just not that interesting. We focus for quite another reason. It is a tool to help us escape useless thinking and unclutter the mind.

Detachment and clarity are the real fruits of meditation. You eventually become able to see anything with dispassion. You see your body, pleasure and pain just as they are. You can watch the play of your thoughts and feelings, almost as if they belong to someone else. You can consciously observe the dramas around you without being sucked into them. At any time, you can choose to be emotionally engaged or detached, or somewhere in between. You may not be able to control your outer life, but at least you can see what is going on and choose your response.

When people meditate on the breath or a mantra, they also watch the body relaxing and the mind becoming freer. It is this process, not the breath or the mantra in itself, that makes meditation so interesting. Shoulders loosen. The breathing becomes softer. Pains surface and release. Bursts of feeling come and go. You 'tick off' thoughts of the day, and are relieved to get clear of them. Moments of insight arise. Dream images or feelings of bodily pleasure come and go.

You may meditate on the breath for years. That part of your practice may never change. Each time you meditate, however, the inner scenery is different. Old preoccupations go and new ones arise. In time, you become more healthy, grounded and clear-minded. The mind continually throws up something new. This is what makes meditation so fascinating. You may seem to be focusing on the breath. In fact, you are watching the entire process unfold around you.

Focusing Is the Basic Skill

Meditation is based on two skills: *focusing* and *watching with detachment* or 'just watching'. These skills are perfectly ordinary, but meditation develops them to a high degree. Focusing means paying attention to the meditation object — be it the breath or a mantra or whatever. Watching with detachment, or 'just watching', means noticing the other thoughts and sensations that tug at the mind, but not reacting to them.

Focusing is a crude, but powerful skill. It is the spadework. Most meditations in this book and elsewhere are about learning to focus. Focusing is the mind-tool that prises us loose from obsessive thought. It is the foundation for 'just watching'. It is also a strong sedative. It slows the metabolic rate down within seconds and leads into the trance states.

Focusing is a simpler skill than watching with detachment. It is easy to understand and it is obvious when you are doing it right. You can check by asking yourself: 'Am I still with the breath?' or 'Am I still saying my mantra?'

'Just Watching' Leads to Detachment

Most meditations emphasise focusing. A few, very few, meditations emphasise the opposite skill. In these, you attempt to 'just watch' the stream of thoughts and sensations flow through you, with perfect detachment. This is also called 'witnessing', or 'being a spectator', or 'observing' or 'bare attention'. The Buddhist word for this practice is *vipassana*, which is usually translated as 'awareness' or 'mindfulness'.

Vipassana literally means 'seeing deeply.' If you see your life and mind with clarity, however, you become wise. So, *vipassana* is also translated as 'insight' because of its results.

Many people make awareness their main meditation. It is the main practice in the Burmese and Thai traditions. Thousands of Westerners have found this the most valuable thing they have learnt from the East.

Awareness means being able to see anything, just as it is, without aversion or attraction. It used to be developed systematically. First, you would watch the sensations and processes of the body objectively. Then you would notice your automatic like and dislike responses to things. After that, you would dispassionately observe your thoughts and emotions come and go.

Focusing is not so important in an awareness meditation. You cultivate detachment instead. Ideally, you don't regard any one thing as more important than any other. Your awareness should be non-selective. The mind becomes like a mirror. You may notice an itch, a thought of tomorrow, a passing motorcycle, a feeling of regret, the heartbeat or a dream image in succession. You notice them, but try to be equally detached towards them all. In practice, you notice when the mind is attaching to something and deliberately pull yourself loose.

Focusing and 'Just Watching' Occur Naturally

Focusing occurs naturally when something interests us. It could be a good book, the taste of a soup or a beautiful person. When we are focused, a minor miracle occurs: the other thoughts stop — they slip into the background. This is why focusing is such a powerful tool. As soon as our mind disengages from the book or the soup or the person, however, the other thoughts resurface.

We use both skills all the time. Thousands of thoughts and sensations flow through the mind each minute. We pay attention to some (i.e. we focus on them), and notice, but ignore, others. Doing paperwork, cleaning the car, buying groceries and even putting on your shoes or worrying, all demand a degree of attention or focus.

For example, we focus on a street directory until we see where to go. Then we focus on starting the car, pulling out into traffic and driving along the road. We focus serially on one thing after another (but not on all at once).

When looking at the directory, we still notice other things: a twinge of back pain, the sound of a distant traffic, a thought about shopping, a memory, a flash of irritation. We notice them, but don't stop looking at the directory. We are focused, and 'just watching' at the same time.

Focusing and 'Just Watching' Naturally Alternate

We practice both these skills at once when we meditate. For example, you try to focus on the breath and let other thoughts arise without engaging them ('I wonder what's on TV tonight? When can I buy some cigarettes? Melanie really is a creep! ...').

Focusing on the breath is simple, and even a little boring. If you stay with it, however, you can extract yourself from the other thoughts. This is why meditation works. Simple as it is, focusing on the breath will relax you much more than thinking at random about TV, cigarettes and Melanie.

It is very rare to focus so deeply that we fail to notice other thoughts and sensations in the background. When we notice one, we actually focus on it for a fraction of a second. This 'momentary focus' won't disturb you so long as it remains momentary. 'Just watching' means watching for just a second and not losing your basic meditation object in doing so.

This momentary focus is quite different from your 'sustained focus' on the meditation object. You may spend a second focused on Melanie or the cigarettes, but six or eight seconds at a time on the breath or the mantra. In a meditation, you usually alternate sustained focus on the object with momentary focus on the rest.

It is almost impossible to focus 'purely' or watch 'purely'. Every meditation involves both. The mind naturally oscillates between the centre and the periphery. It focuses on the breath for a few seconds, then goes on border patrol. It checks out background thoughts and sensations, just to reassure itself everything is okay, then returns to the breath, and so on.

Focusing is the art of escape. By focusing on one thing, you pull away from all the rest. 'Just watching', however, is the art of love. It is to be able to accept fully, or tolerate, anything that arises, just as it is, without being distracted by it.

Good Focus Depends on 'Just Watching' and Vice Versa

When you are well focused, you feel good. The mind settles into the object and the body palpably relaxes. 'Just watching', however, may not be so pleasant. You often notice thoughts and sensations that irritate you, and you wish they weren't there. As a result, meditators often try hard to focus and block out everything else, but they are bound to fail. Their strategy is wrong. This grim determination may be morally admirable, but it rarely succeeds.

Focusing actually depends on the opposite skill of 'just watching'. You may try to focus on the breath, for example, but an insistent thought or sensation is tugging you. This is the time to drop focusing and practice 'just watching'. Once you name the distraction, it often loses its power over you and you can return to the breath easily. In any meditation, notice when 'just watching' is more appropriate than focusing, and vice versa.

Distractions actually need their moment on stage to move on. We can't just lock them in the dungeon and hope they die. 'Just watching', not 'trying harder', is the key to good focus. In other words, don't hold tight to the object. Just let go of everything else.

Awareness Develops in Five Stages

Some thoughts and sensations are easy to detach from — a slight headache or traffic noise outside. Others are more demanding — thoughts about the day, planning this and that. Some have strong emotional hooks — you may be in conflict with someone or want something badly. Some are deep-seated, chronic and barely conscious — a persistent health problem or the pain of a bitter divorce.

They arise, one by one, as you focus on the breath. It is quite a challenge to notice them (usually you can't help it) and let them pass. Each is individual. You may wish you could just ignore them, or 'get rid of them', but this rarely works. Being able to notice them with a clear mind is the best way to break their power over you.

It is easy for me to say 'Just watch what arises, and let it all pass.' The practice of it is not that simple. We actually develop awareness in five stages, and none of them is particularly easy. The five stages are: noticing, detaching, tolerating, accepting and insight.

The first stage, noticing, is actually to notice what has caught your attention. We can be irritable without knowing why. We are often distracted by thoughts and sensations that are not quite conscious. The first stage is to say 'Hang on! What am I doing here?' and be able to identify the thought or distraction.

The second stage, detaching, occurs when you can see clearly what is draining your energy away. If you can name it — for example, 'shoulder pain' or 'Josephine' — you are detaching from it. Detachment doesn't happen instantly. Usually an unwanted thought or sensation has you in its grip at first. Detaching is like pulling out of an unwanted embrace, or picking hooks out of your flesh.

The third stage, tolerating, is where the distraction remains, but no longer upsets your meditation. It still requires a little vigilance. The headache, the sadness, the problem at work may remain in your consciousness, but you can still focus on the breath and relax. We may tolerate a distraction, but still dislike it. This keeps us slightly on edge.

The fourth stage, acceptance, usually occurs when you are deeply relaxed. The heart opens and we find we are completely at ease in the moment, just as it is. This is when the shoulder pain or the difficulties at work cease to be pain at all. They become just inescapable parts of our environment, like the weather.

Acceptance is quite an art. It takes time to accept ourselves just as we are — our failures, our inability to meditate the way we want, our less-than-perfect bodies and less-than-perfect lives and personalities. When meditating, we stop trying to manipulate ourselves and the world. For a few minutes at least, we live in a state of love.

Acceptance leads to the last stage, insight. When our mind is clear of aversion and desire, we can actually look at the distraction and understand it. We have come full circle. First we had to pull away from it. Now we can look at it with a clear mind.

For example, we can stand back from the pain of a remembered argument. The bigger picture then becomes obvious. We see the ingredients — the words, the flush of irrational anger or sadness, the preceding causes, our tendency to react in certain ways, the clash of personalities. When we see it in perspective, it is usually not as important as it seemed to be.

This is understanding. It can occur in a flash and release the emotional tension immediately. As the Vipassana teacher Larry Rosenberg says, 'When [awareness] touches things, they're less problematic, or not a problem at all. It's magical.' This spontaneous understanding is called *insight* in the Buddhist tradition. This is the purpose of the ten-day Vipassana retreats found all around the world.

Awareness Is a State of Mind

Thoughts are very seductive. 'Just watching' them is not easy. We can often fool ourselves — instead of 'momentarily' focusing on a distraction, we stay longer than a moment. We are tempted to think about it a little. Before long, we can be drifting from thought to thought, while pretending we are 'just watching' them.

Watching is watching. It is not thinking. When we recognise this clear, detached, mirror-like mind state, we can switch into it any time we want. A student of mine, who has to deal with customer complaints, often uses it in his work. He says, he 'just watches' an irate customer rave until they've talked themselves out. Only then does he respond.

Most people don't practise awareness as such. They use it as an adjunct to a focusing meditation. They may slip into a few minutes of awareness in the midst of a body-scanning or mantra meditation, for example. They examine a patch of mental turbulence to get clear of it or they cultivate this detached, watching mind during the day. Awareness is as much a quality of mind as a meditation practice.

MEDITATION: AWARENESS

In most meditations you focus inwards on the meditation object. This practice does the opposite. You focus outwards, 'just watching' the passing thoughts and sensations. You are practising detachment — learning to sit and watch the show, without getting involved.

For stability, you still need a basic meditation object, but you hold it lightly. You hold the breath, for example, while also noticing other thoughts and sensations arise. You both look 'inwards' to the breath, and 'outwards' to the periphery. Every few seconds, you name the most obvious thought or sensation, like taking an inventory.

It can be useful to see the mind as a river, or a 'stream of consciousness', and our thoughts and sensations as debris floating down this river. Often the debris is ugly — aluminium cans, plastic bags, a bloated cow or two. None of this matters, so long as we stay on the bank and just watch. Every few seconds we 'name' the most obvious thing: 'sore knee ... hungry ... TV ... out-breath ... money ... birds ...'.

Our problem comes when we plunge into the river and grab on to this or that. Soon we are lurching from one thing to another, and being swept downstream. If a thought has caught you, let it go, throw it back in the stream and clamber back to the breath.

The breath, or any other meditation object, anchors you. The breath is your seat from which you watch the river. When you fall into the river, then forget the naming and find your way back to the seat. Ideally you should spend at least 25 to 50 per cent of the time well focused on the breath, and the rest 'just watching'.

Eventually, like a mirror, the mind becomes capable of reflecting all things equally. It doesn't recoil from an ugly sound, reach out towards a beautiful feeling or ignore the trivia. It is peaceful and undisturbed, regardless of the thoughts and sensations passing by.

Something curious and delightful often happens with this meditation. There can be fewer distracting thoughts than usual. Often people battle with thoughts in a meditation. In this practice, however, because you are waiting for thoughts to arise, they often don't come.

MEDITATION — AWARENESS (continued)

The nature of thoughts is to be sneaky. They prefer to grab you from behind and drag you away. If you wait for them, they can't ambush you.

Instructions

Relax the body and focus on the breath (or any other meditation object). Establish your seat before you attempt to watch the parade. During the meditation be with the breath at least 25 to 50 per cent of the time.

While focusing on the breath, notice what else is in consciousness. Become a dispassionate observer. Don't go out and search for anything. Things will arise without any effort on your part. If nothing arises, enjoy the emptiness. Stay centred on the meditation object as much as you like. Every few seconds, 'name' the dominant thought or sensation in the mind. You can name:

- sensations: 'pain ... traffic ... breathing ...';
- the content of thoughts: 'food ... work ... Peter ...'; or
- emotions or mind states: 'bored ... angry ... sleepy ...'.

Don't try to name everything — if you did, you would be very busy. Just name the big ones. Notice how nice things attract you and unpleasant things repulse you. Be careful not to be subtly interested in what you see. If you are, you are falling into the river. Don't be annoyed with what arises. In this meditation, nothing is a distraction. Anything is grist for the mill. Cultivate a bland, clear, watching mind.

If you suspect you are lost, you probably are. Don't continue naming. Just return to the breath. Alternatively, ask yourself:

- 'Where am I?' (or 'Where is the mind right now?'); or
- 'What is this?' (or 'What am I thinking about?').

Don't forget the breath. Keep going back to it. After naming for a while, you may find you just want to stay with the breath and enjoy that stillness. Don't feel you have to go out and explore. Conserve your energy. Do as little as possible.

CHAPTER 8

Mantra

In the introduction, I said there were four meditations that were more important than the rest. These are the breath, body scanning, awareness and mantra. Awareness, the subject of the last chapter, is the most subtle. Now we come to mantra, which is the simplest. It is so simple that it is rarely 'taught' at all. You are usually told 'Here, say this mantra' and off you go with it.

A mantra is a word or phrase that you say, over and over, often in time with the breath. It is like an affirmation or a silent chant. Unlike an affirmation, however, a mantra may have no meaning at all. The sounds and rhythm of the syllables are more important than any meaning they may have.

Mantra are musical. Each one has its individual rhythm and sound quality. They are like very short musical phrases, or chants, and people do frequently sing them. They are a more sensual, hypnotic and colourful practice than affirmations.

Mantra is a word from Sanskrit (the holy language of India) which means, literally, 'mind-tool'. In other words, a mantra is something for the mind to hold on to. Here are some common mantra:

- OM
- RAM
- OM AH HUNG
- HAMSA (and its opposite, SOHAM)
- SHALOM
- OM MANI PEME HUNG
- OM NAMAH SHIVAYA
- HARE KRISHNA

Mantra can be used in many ways because they are so simple. Usually, people sit quietly with their eyes closed, saying or 'thinking' their mantra like a silent chant. Some people, however, say it out loud.

Hindus often sing their mantra. Hinduism also has a great tradition of popular sacred songs (called *kirtan* or *bhajan*). These beautiful songs are often very simple and repetitive. People will sing them for hours, and the boundaries between song and mantra become indistinguishable.

Mantra often have a devotional component. The mantra can be the names of various gods. When some Christians learn meditation, they often feel an affinity for mantra. The 'Hail Marys', the use of rosary beads and the repetitive liturgies of the Church are very similar to the way some Hindus use mantra.

People often dance to their mantra, as we know from seeing the 'Hare Krishnas' in the streets. It takes a lot of energy to sing and dance a mantra, so this is regarded as good for young, undisciplined minds.

In India, mantra are also said very quickly and loudly. You occasionally see a holy man — usually a young one — marching through the street loudly shouting his mantra. This is the high-pressure hose theory of mantra. It blasts everything else out of consciousness.

People often start saying a mantra out loud. As they relax, the mantra may fade to a murmur and dissolve into the background hum of the body. Often the mantra stops of its own accord and the person rests in stillness. In the deepest states, there can be no words at all, not even mantra.

The Historical Background

Of all the practices in this book, mantra carries the most mystical baggage. Mantra comes from that 'abracadabra' era in human prehistory when sounds were believed to have magical effects. The mythology is that each sound has a unique vibration which can trigger off effects in our bodies and in the world around us.

The earliest Indian holy texts are basically collections of mantra or spells. There are mantra to make the sun rise, or the rains fall, to protect you from disease, to ensure the favour of the gods, to make your cows fertile and your neighbour's cows barren, to destroy your enemies and to make your neighbour's wife fall in love with you. Who said that meditation wasn't useful?

The spells, of course, must be said exactly right to be effective. From this, a whole priestly caste arose. They were the specialists in mantra and the associated magical practices and sacrifices. We can be grateful for them. Even today, thousands of them said the correct mantra to ensure the sun came up this morning.

As usual, there is a grain of truth in all of this. Sounds do have individual effects. The mantra 'Ah', for example, is like a sigh. It drops through the body. If you said it thousands of times, you would become as loose as a beanbag. It is a meaningless sound, but it still has an effect.

The mantra 'Hung' is stronger. It resonates in the chest, like a bell. It is a 'seal' syllable. It holds in the energy. In contrast, the mantra 'Hree!' is more zingy. It seems to shoot upwards and lift your energy. It is clearly not intended to make you relax.

Each mantra, therefore, will have a slightly different rhythm, mood and general effect. Different religious schools often identify with certain mantra, like a badge or a slogan. They often claim their favourite mantra has unique effects, better than all the rest. I suspect this is just the blindness of a lover.

Mantra 'Without Trappings'

Although mantra often have no meaning, they may have associations. The 'Hare Krishna' mantra may bring to mind Krishna making love to the cowgirls. 'Om mani peme hung' is the Tibetan mantra of friendliness towards all beings. 'Om namah Shivaya' evolves one's inner wisdom and power, symbolised by the god Shiva.

These associations can be useful. On the other hand, they can make mantra seem too religious and even superstitious. Both Westerners and Asians have attempted to strip mantra back to its chant-like essence. Chanting works well. Every culture uses it. Almost any word would suffice. You certainly don't need a mantra sanctified by thousands of years of culture and tradition.

Benson, in *The Relaxation Response*, suggests using the word 'one' as a mantra. LeShan, in the old book *How To Meditate,* suggests finding a two-syllable mantra by opening the telephone book at random. You take the first syllable of the first name, then open the book again and repeat the process. You have a mantra! Rational as this seems, I find people still prefer the traditional mantra.

The Transcendental Meditation (TM) group came out of India in about 1960. Its members insist that meditation is a no-nonsense psycho-physical discipline. They fund research into the effects of meditation and have largely succeeded making meditation seem respectable in the West. TM lends itself to scientific testing because the practice is very standardised. Like McDonalds hamburgers, it is the same all around the world. Most of the independent research on meditation has been done on TM for precisely this reason.

Nonetheless, TM has cleverly exploited the magical associations of traditional mantra. Since each sound has a unique vibratory effect in your body, they argue you must use the combination of sounds that is just right for you. They don't say what would happen if you said the wrong sounds. (Perhaps you would go insane, or your liver would explode!)

Fortunately, they happen to be the experts in such things. For a few hundred dollars (the price is negotiable), they will give you your personalised mantra in an initiation ceremony. You are forbidden to tell it to anyone, and you meditate on nothing else from that time on (unless you sign up for graduate courses).

So is TM a con? Their technique is good. Despite their hype, it is just an ordinary mantra practice. It probably works well for that third of the population that is temperamentally suited to mantra practice. What price can you put on peace of mind? Many TM practitioners have got their money's worth a thousand times over. If it is expensive, people are more likely to practise and therefore get good results.

Do mantra need, however, to be personalised and secret? In the East, mantra are in the public domain. The most famous mantra are on walls and clothing, in books, and heard in the streets and temples. They are in popular songs and on the front of buses. They are engraved on rocks and flutter from flags. Kids know them before they can read. There is also the myth that the more people there are who use a mantra, the more powerful it becomes.

Millions of people are using mantra this very minute. It is a very popular and effective practice. TM practitioners are therefore in complete isolation in saying that you need a personal mantra. This belief also flies in the face of the evidence. Millions of people over thousands of years have had excellent results using 'ordinary' mantra.

Most people who know anything about meditation look askance at TM's emphasis on a personal mantra. It has all the appearance of a marketing ploy used to justify the high price. Usually the only people who find TM's arguments plausible are those who are completely new to meditation and so have nothing with which to compare it. Personally, I don't believe in 'magical' meditation objects. I feel most of the effect of a meditation comes from the relaxed and alert quality of mind, not from the object itself.

Mantra and the breath meditation are the two most widely used meditations in the world. Most people have an immediate affinity for one or the other, though they frequently use both in time. The breath meditation is more cool, analytical and down-to-earth. It leads to clarity of mind. Mantra, despite the efforts of many to demystify it, is still more emotive and imaginative. This is just the nature of mantra.

Mantra is an exceptionally simple practice at heart. It is just a quiet chant that sets up a flow of sound within you. The images and meanings that can go with it can be useful. Or they can clutter the mind. It is better not to regard mantra as a magical, or spiritually exalted, incantation. It is really just a 'tool for the mind'—something for the mind to hold on to, just like the breath.

MEDITATION: 'HAMSA'

There are at least four distinct ways of meditating on the breath. First, you can simply sense the movement of the breath within you, without any words. Secondly, you could count the breaths, just to make sure the mind is not drifting away. Thirdly, you could use the flow of a mantra to support the mind. Finally you could say an affirmation such as 'Let go' or 'Peace' as you breathe.

There are many two-syllable mantra. They fit the breathing easily: one syllable on the in-breath, one on the outbreath. Generally you breathe normally and let the syllables follow the breath. If the breath is long, you stretch out the mantra. If it is short, you contract it. A word of warning: if you try to breathe too evenly, you can hyperventilate.

Two-syllable mantras tend to make the breathing more regular anyway. This has its advantages. Any kind of rhythmic activity — swimming, knitting, walking, singing — is soothing to the mind. It counteracts the jumpy, grasshopper nature of thinking.

'Hamsa' is a sensuous mantra. You say 'ham-' on the in-breath and '-sa' on the out-breath. The '-sa' is like a sigh. If you want, you can imagine your body being hollow — the mantra is like a wave that ebbs and flows within you. Or you can massage the body with the sound. First, you say the sounds. Then the sounds can take over and carry you.

A mantra is a meditation object like any other. The same rules apply. Focus on the mantra. When the mind wanders off, bring it back. Let other thoughts and sensations pass by in the background. Usually you say your mantra while still noticing other things. Mantra doesn't block out the rest of the world.

MEDITATION: 'OM MANI PEME HUNG'

Unlike the 'hamsa' mantra, most mantra are not synchronised with the breath. As your breath gets lighter, the mind can often drift away from two-syllable mantra. Most of the famous mantra are between five and ten syllables long. This gives you plenty to get your teeth into, and they often have a good rhythm as well.

MEDITATION: 'OM MANI PEME HUNG' (continued)

Perhaps the most famous of all is the Tibetan six-syllable mantra 'Om mani peme hung'. This seems to consist of four little words. It is usually said as a three-beat, however, with the accents on the second, fourth and sixth syllables: 'Om *ma*-ni *pe*-me *hung*, om *ma*-ni *pe*-me *hung*' and so on. It is usually said rather fast, with no pauses, and as a continuous patter, unrelated to the breath.

The formal spelling is 'Om mani padme hum' and it is often pronounced this way. Meditators, however, generally slur the edges, so that it rolls along better: 'Omanipaymayhung, omanipaymayhung,' and so on.

This has a lovely rolling triplet beat to it. It becomes a continuous flow of sound with an upbeat, energising feel. One student said it is like sitting in a train and hearing the rhythm of the wheels on the tracks.

It is possible to say the mantra in time with the breath, but very few people do. It loses the forward momentum which is so much part of its character. A few people, myself included, do it with the heartbeat. It is most usually said as a continuous hum, independent of heartbeat or breath. Tibetans often say it quietly but out loud. They may say it while working, while walking or in any circumstances at all. When they are gathered in a temple, it creates a lovely humming sound, like thousands of bees. Within your body, the mantra creates a continuous hum, like a bass note of sound, that is easy to hold on to — and to find your way back to if you lose it.

This mantra tends to have associations rather than meaning. It is a 'heart-opening' mantra. It is designed to evoke the feeling of non-specific friendliness towards all beings. You can imagine your heart opening like a flower and the warm pink light of love and acceptance spreading — first through your own body and then out to others (see chapter 18, pages 142–143).

This mantra could be seen as the national anthem of Tibet. The Dalai Lama says, 'My religion is kindness', and this mantra is said to be the vibration of that mind state. It is the mantra of 'Peace, love and goodwill towards all beings'.

CHAPTER 9

Affirmations

An affirmation is a word or a phrase that you say repeatedly through the meditation, often in time with the breath. Like counting, this gives the mind something to do, so it doesn't wander off the path. An affirmation is like a mantra, but carries more verbal meaning. Like a silent chant, it often has a soothing and slightly hypnotic effect.

Affirmations 'use a thorn to extract a thorn'. They use words to stop words. The continuous flow of sound jams the airwaves, as it were, and stops other thoughts taking hold.

Here are some simple affirmations:

* SLOW DOWN
* LET GO
* PEACE AND LOVE
* RELAX
* LET IT BE
* BE STILL

It is best to find your own affirmations. Any word or phrase that evokes a good feeling would do. People often say one of the names of God. If you enjoyed your recent holiday in Bali, then you could use the word 'Bali'. You could perhaps say the name of an absent lover or grandchild. A line of poetry or a single phrase of a song would suffice. Some people recite longer texts, like the Lord's prayer, or the uplifting ideas in self-help books.

You may like the breath meditation, but find counting too bland and emotionally neutral. You can add more colour by saying an affirmation instead of counting. An affirmation can be like a mini-instruction to yourself, reminding you where you are going.

Affirmations can set a mood quickly, and rapidly shoehorn you into meditation. They are also ideal as spot meditations. If you are getting uptight at work, you could easily cool down by saying 'let go' a few times as you breathe.

What Kind of Affirmation Is Best?

So which kind of affirmation is best? A short one or a long one? A simple one or a beautiful and spiritually uplifting one? It depends on what you want to do. Complex ones, perhaps with an accompanying visualisation, are good if you want to shape your way of thinking. Simple ones, however, are better if you want to relax deeply and clear the mind.

Meditation is ideally a 'word-free' zone. You try to shift away from thinking into the sensations of the present. Affirmations are in the middle, somewhere between thinking and sensing. They involve words, but very few of them. They don't rabbit on the way our thoughts usually do. By repeating affirmations hundreds of times, they can become rhythmic and chant-like. Ideally, they set a background mood, like wallpaper or ambient music, rather than stimulate thought.

Many people, of course, do use their affirmation as a springboard for contemplation. They deliberately weave thoughts, feelings and images around their affirmation. This is a classical Western-style meditation. While people using their affirmation in this way may relax, and in doing so evoke a good mood, this is still a kind of thinking. Pleasant, well-directed thoughts are obviously better than unpleasant ones, but they still keep the mind quite active. The body will not be as relaxed, nor the mind as clear, as they might be.

Affirmations relax you well if they are simple and chant-like. Their meaning is actually secondary. Anything rhythmic, such as singing, dancing or running, soothes the mind and extracts it from the complexity of thought. Chanting a word, for example, is much simpler than thinking about its meaning.

Although an affirmation has meaning, the less you think about, the deeper you relax.

The Western Tradition

Many people use an affirmation as a pep-talk to 'program' the mind, or to give instructions from the ego to the subconscious. They contemplate its meaning to reshape their attitudes. Some use affirmations as magical spells, to 'manifest' what they want in the outer world. This is a particularly Western approach. Let me explain how it came about.

First, 'meditation' is not a good word to describe the skills I teach here. In the English language, *meditating* means 'to think deeply' or 'contemplate'. A person facing a difficult issue may say 'I'll go away and meditate on that.' This is an accurate use of the word. Meditation in this Western sense of 'deep thinking', however, only becomes meditation in the Eastern sense when it moves beyond thought into direct non-verbal awareness.

St Benedict, in the Middle Ages, described three stages of meditation. The first involved reciting a line of scripture, like an affirmation, to anchor the mind. The second involved contemplating its meaning and seeing its significance in your life. This could involve imagination and visualisation. The third involved leaving words and thought behind, and dropping into a passive space he called 'divine listening'. In this state, you waited for inner wisdom to arise, or for God or the angels to speak to you.

People who entered this third, non-verbal state often found they no longer needed the guidance of the Catholic Church. They contacted God, or their inner voice, directly. The Church, however, saw itself as the essential intermediary between God and man. It did not want to be side-lined by meditators going directly to the source. So it proscribed deep meditation as dangerous, since it often led to heresy. From the Middle Ages onwards, lay people were forbidden by the Church to enter the deep states.

Meditators were regarded as the 'pagans in our midst'. Hundreds of thousands were slaughtered as heretics, long before the witch-hunts of central Europe killed off another ten million people. Great mystics, such as Meister Eckhardt and St John of the Cross, always ran the risk of imprisonment and death, and their books were banned by the Catholic Church until the twentieth century.

In the paranoid climate of the Reformation in 1578, the Catholic Church banned the deep states of meditation even for the clergy. Since the

Protestant churches had no strong contemplative tradition anyway, deep meditation effectively vanished from mainstream Western society.

What was still allowed, however, was St Benedict's first two stages. For four centuries, Western 'meditation' has revolved around the contemplation of scripture, chanting (which leads to affirmations), prayer (or 'talking to God') and visualisation. This was less spontaneous, more like ordinary thought and more controllable. St Ignatius, the founder of the Jesuit order, said meditation was an act of will. You used prayer and visualisation to make yourself a better person, and to overcome the evil tendencies of your mind.

The Secular and New Age Use of Affirmations

By the mid-1800s, meditation again broke free of Church control, mostly in North America. Even though meditation rapidly became secular, it modified the existing Christian practices which, of course, excluded the deeper non-verbal states. Consequently, modern Western and New Age meditations are strongly based on the use of words (affirmations) and visualisation, and the exercise of the will to shape consciousness.

Mary Baker Eddy, the founder of Christian Science, taught that if your thoughts were healthy, your body would be, too. In other words, your mind creates your physical health or ill health. Norman Vincent Peale taught the 'power of positive thinking', whereby good things would happen to you if you believed they would. Other teachers talk about 'manifesting', where by visualising your goals you make them happen.

Obviously, there is some sense in this, but it is often pushed to extremes. Although described in psychological terms, it is good to remember it arose in the context of religious groups. It often involves a strange cocktail of self-hypnosis, religious faith, sympathetic magic and blind hope. And while, to the annoyance of skeptics, it often works well for some, these people are definitely in the minority.

About a quarter of the population are suggestible, or hypnotic, types. Such people are natural believers. This has a bad side: they can be easily led. It also has a good side. Some of them can change their mind state quite readily by positive thinking and appropriate imagery. In the most dramatic cases, they can cure themselves of serious illness.

Most people, however, do not respond to words or images that fully. They are too rational. They may try, but it rarely works—it is just not their temperament. Telling such people that positive thoughts will cure their cancer (and implying that their negative thoughts have made them sick) is very tactless. It is a modern version of the old superstition that the sick and unfortunate deserved their fate because of their mental depravity.

In the East, affirmations and visualisations are regarded as preliminaries which can be skipped altogether. It is not hard to drop below the surface of words and thoughts in a minute once you know how. The deep states are simple and clear. Meditations involving words, thoughts and images are fussy in comparison.

Affirmations are a kind of 'deep thinking', but a shallow meditation. Because you 'think' using images and feeling as well as words, this is more powerful than ordinary thinking. Since we all have to think at times, it is good to be able to think in this more contemplative zone.

There are many books of encouraging affirmations and spiritual reflections. These can be very useful. If you sit quietly and say to yourself repeatedly: 'I am a warm and loving person, who moves with grace and ease', you can reinforce those qualities in yourself and counteract their opposites. This is meditation in the sense of 'contemplating deeply'. At a certain point, however, it is good to stop thinking, let go the words and drop into an inner space. In this way, you follow St Benedict's three stages:

1. Reciting the phrase.
2. Contemplating the meaning deeply.
3. 'Divine listening' (or waiting with a clear mind).

MEDITATION: AFFIRMATIONS

Affirmations are chant-like and can be a little hypnotic. This is why they work. The words and meaning are secondary, but still important. Choose an affirmation that evokes a good feeling for you. If your affirmation is longer than two or three words, still try to say it rhythmically in time with the breath, if possible.

Instructions

- Relax the body and breathing as usual. Tune into the natural ebb and flow of the breath. Now say the words 'Slow down' in time with the breath. Say the word 'slow' on the in-breath, and 'down' on the out-breath.
- Let the words follow the natural breath. If the breath is long, stretch out the words. If it is short, you have a short affirmation. Don't try to make the breathing deep or regular.
- Weave the words and the breath together. Let them carry you along. If you wish, you can imagine the breath like a wave that ebbs and flows, from your feet to the crown of your head, and back again.
- Let the breathing slow down naturally. Follow the breath to the very end, and rest there. Don't hurry the in-breath. Let it come in its own time. Feel the mind slowing down, becoming soft and attentive to the breath.
- If you wish, change to another affirmation. Say the words 'Let go' in time with the breath. You may find it has a different effect on you. Over time, experiment with different affirmations to see what suits you.

CHAPTER 10

Shifting from Thinking to Sensing

Most of us think too much. Thoughts keep us awake at night. We may worry, plan, analyse, comment and reflect continuously, as an automatic habit. These inner conversations can be satisfying, but are often exasperating. As the Bhagavad Gita, the sacred Hindu text, says, 'there is no end to thought'. So there is little point in trying to 'think it all through'.

Our thoughts affect our bodies instantly. We soon notice this when we meditate. Certain thoughts speed us up, while other thoughts wind us down. Our thoughts are like the tail that wags the dog. Some words or images act like caffeine. They put us on red alert instantly. Others are like sedatives, dissolving our tension in seconds.

Pleasant or not, thoughts are exhausting. The brain consumes a quarter of the body's energy each day. Many of my students complain: 'I just want to switch my thoughts off.' It is so hard to do. One man said, 'I just want to put a bullet through it all.'

Though we may try to stop thoughts, we rarely succeed. The bad news is that thoughts never stop. If you wake someone who was sleeping and ask what they were doing, they will usually respond: 'I was thinking of something.'

The good news, however, is that you don't have to respond to thoughts. It is said that you can't stop birds flying overhead, but you can stop them nesting in your hair. As you can't stop thoughts, however, what do you do?

The strategy seems ridiculously simple. We become more sensual. We shepherd our attention away from thought into the world of sight, sound, smell, taste or touch. We consciously look at a painting, we taste the cake, we feel the sensations of the body.

You may ask, 'So, all I need to do is stop thinking about my problems and look at the tree outside? Is that all?' The answer is 'yes'. Just do it better. Look more deeply. Enjoy it. You are bound to relax. When looking at the tree, you stop feeding your habitual thoughts and the mind can rest.

Beta and Alpha Brainwaves

When we relax, the body chemistry changes. There are also dramatic changes in the brain. These are not as easy to observe unless you are wired up to an electro-encephalograph (ECG), but it is good to know about them.

The brain emits electrical impulses continuously. The shift to sensing changes our brainwaves within seconds. When you are thinking, the brain waves are fast and unrhythmic. These are called *beta* brainwaves, and they look like choppy water on a graph. Their agitated, jumping lines even look like the way we think. The beta waves are between 14 and 30 cycles a second.

When we relax or shift into sensing mode, the brain waves settle down. They become bigger, slower and rhythmic. It is quite lovely to see them on a graph. They even look serene. These are called *alpha* brain waves, and are between 7 and 13 cycles per minute.

In the beta state, we think. In alpha, we sense things. In beta, we are tense. In alpha we relax. During the day, we alternate between alpha and beta states. Their functions are complementary. We need both, but we tend to overdo beta and ignore alpha.

Beta is an active, thinking, responsive mind state. It is busy. We are in beta most of our waking day. Beta enables us to think, talk, handle many different stimuli at once and speculate about past and future events. Beta revs us up, through the activities of adrenalin and cortisol and other hormones. It is also associated with the left side of the brain, which handles analytical, linear, critical thought.

If you notice the feeling behind your thoughts, you will find they are usually fuelled by low-grade chronic fear, anger or desire. You may be afraid things are not going to work out well or you may be angry with what is happening. Perhaps it is that you feel you must have or get something, or you won't be happy. This is our everyday self-orientated drip-feed of fear, anger and desire.

When in the beta state, we are burning energy. But the reserves are limited. At some point, we feel tired and start thinking of a tea break. The mind naturally wants to drop into alpha — a relaxed, sensing, inactive state—to rejuvenate itself. If we ignore this impulse and push on, the mind often switches off anyway. Despite our best endeavours, we go into a mentally dull space — often about late morning or two o'clock in the afternoon.

Ideally, alpha and beta alternate on 90-minute cycles right through the day and night. Our energy expenditure is regulated like a thermostat. It rises, peaks, falls, recovers and rises again. If you tend to wake up at night, you may notice that it occurs 90 minutes or 3 hours after you fell asleep. This is when the energy cycle is peaking again.

The alpha state is the mirror opposite to beta, and is therefore its natural antidote. We are producing alpha waves when we are relaxed or in sensing mode. When sensing outweighs thinking — when biting into an apple or listening to falling rain—we are shifting into alpha. When we feel an emotion 'in our guts', rather than verbalising it, we are in alpha.

Alpha is passive. It is a state of 'just being' rather than 'doing'. It is intellectually simpler, but more 'grounded', than beta. You may not sparkle verbally, but you know where you are and what you feel. It conserves rather than spends energy. It is nourishing. You feel the body and mind repairing themselves.

Beta and Alpha Alternate Rapidly

We switch between thinking and sensing very rapidly. If you are talking with a friend, you will be in beta. You may try to simultaneously listen to some music in the background. You won't, however, be able to get into it. The brain is in thinking, not sensing, mode. If you said to your friend, 'Let's listen to the music', the difficulty would vanish. Within seconds, the brain adjusts to alpha and you can take in the music fully.

You bite an apple and the taste floods your being. You are right there, sensing, in alpha and in the moment. Yet a moment later, you think, 'These are great apples. I'll buy some more tomorrow.' You are no longer tasting the apple, and you are drifting back into beta.

Just Be More Sensual

We don't need to sit for half an hour a day in formal meditation. That is just practice. It's not the real thing. It is like doing the scales and never playing the music. All we really need is to spend more time sensing, and less time thinking.

I suspect meditators are happy not because they have found peace, but because they enjoy the sense world more. During the day, they have more gaps between the words. They taste their food, they feel the morning wind on their face, they notice the sunset and they enjoy the touch of another human being a little more than most.

Formal meditation has lovely after-effects. It means the mind is a little slower and more deliberate. It lingers with things more. It is not at the mercy of thoughts, and can slip into alpha easily.

Like most of my students, my days are busy. Before the evening classes, I like to walk in Kings Park. I watch the native birds flit through the flame trees, sipping the nectar. I feel the moisture in the air after a winter shower. I watch the sun's rays flash out from clouds.

I think these are the best moments of the day. They feel timeless, even though I know I will soon cross the road and be back at work. It feels like I am reaping the rewards of a quarter-century of meditation just by walking for a few minutes in a park at sunset.

MEDITATION: MUSIC

Music is an excellent meditation object. It is usually easy to focus on music — it is entertaining. It calls your attention and leads you along from moment to moment. If you lose it, it is easy to drop back into it.

Nonetheless, music is a meditation object, like any other, and the same principles apply. You mentally put a fence around the music and explore it. You notice when the mind has jumped the fence, and you bring it back. Pleasant as it may be, there is still some discipline involved.

Many of us use music as muzak. We use it to fuzz out the background, or we drift aimlessly along with it, letting our thoughts go where they wish. This may be relaxing, but it won't lead to much mental clarity.

Meditating to music should be more like going to a concert. If we spend $40 on a ticket, we want to hear what we have paid for. We don't want to sit down for two hours and space out. And we find, if we listen to the music carefully, we actually enjoy it more. We pick up detail and colour we would normally miss.

There are stages of depth in listening to music. Initially, the music seems to be distant from us. After a while, however, the music breaks through our mental chatter and we feel in touch with it.

Quite rapidly, it can raise feeling and mood within us. Some people get images and associations. These are not distractions. They are part of the whole experience. Just notice, however, if you are going off at a tangent. Ask yourself occasionally: 'Am I still with the music?' and answer this question honestly.

Occasionally, we become so absorbed in the music we are aware of nothing else. We forget ourselves completely, just for a few seconds. It can be a shock when it is over and we return to the room. This is called a state of 'oneness' or 'absorption'. Enjoy it if it happens.

People often assume you need spacey New Age music in order to meditate. This misses the point. We spend most of our lives trying, with various degrees of frustration, to reorganise the outer world so

MEDITATION: MUSIC (continued)

we can feel good. It is a vain endeavour. Meditation works on the opposite principle. It is the focusing, not the music, that makes us relax. You don't even have to like the music.

So, almost any music will do, as long as it holds your attention. Recently, a man told me, without a trace of irony, that he meditates to the frenetic jazz of John Coltrane. I also like complex music. Bartok string quartets are ideal for me. The music could be fast or slow, tranquil or passionate, simple or complex, classical or New Age or planetary. It is your choice.

Vocal music is often unsuitable because the words get you thinking. Some relaxation music is too fluffy and insubstantial, like candy floss. This may be good for background atmosphere, but too vague for meditation. You need something clear enough to focus on so that you know whether or not you've wandered away from it.

Instructions

- Scan your posture and breathing for a minute or so. Get your mind into alpha before the music starts.
- Switch on the music and enjoy it. Let it resonate in your body. Feel the detail and colour. If images arise, weave them into the meditation.
- Ask yourself occasionally: 'Am I still with the music?' Notice how your mind comes and goes. Notice the special 'live' quality of those moments when you are 100 per cent with the music.
- When the music stops, come back to yourself. Did you relax fully or are you a little charged up? Are you holding your breath or is it soft and loose? When you feel fully in touch with yourself, come out of the meditation.

CHAPTER 11

Having a Dreadful Meditation

Sometimes we have meditations where we can't seem to focus for a moment. 'I can't count more than a single breath before I'm gone,' said one student. Sometimes, one huge obsession dominates us. At other times, thousands of petty concerns drag us this way and that. The unresolved debris of the day agitates the mind and mocks our attempt to focus and relax.

If you are meditating with others, it seems even worse. You look around the room and everyone else seems so calm and serene. They are obviously meditating beautifully. *I must be the only one who can't do it*, you think to yourself.

Afterwards, you may decide that meditation is impossible for you. Your life is too demanding. Trying to relax is just too hard. If only you were on holiday, away from work and the kids, then maybe you could focus properly. People often say 'I know meditation is good for me, but I'll try again when my life has settled down.'

It is good to meditate, however, while you are in hell. It helps you stay cool. Good meditations aren't always pleasant. Meditation will help if you are sick, exhausted, overworked or under emotional pressure. It will help if you are facing a difficult decision, undergoing a life change or are subject to panic attacks or depression. You won't attain perfect peace in twenty minutes, any more than you can recover instantly from an illness. You can, however, make a big shift in the right direction.

Even a 'bad' meditation will slow the mind down and give you some detachment. Afterwards, you may notice your anxiety level has dropped from 'red alert' to merely 'aroused'. This is a healthy change. You may have been panicky. Now you are just miserable. This is physically a more relaxed state. You have achieved something positive. Even though the medicine was bitter — and you'll have to take more of it — you can already feel the benefits.

Even good meditators have chaotic meditations. If you have the average busy modern life, you can expect at least one meditation in three or four to be messy. If you have overloaded yourself, a meditation can't instantly clear the stormy skies, but it can help you can find balance. Since few of us have perfectly peaceful lives, we don't have perfect meditations. Knowing this, don't criticise yourself when you seem to fail.

Often the 'worst' meditations are the most useful. They help you shovel out the garbage. The process may not be much fun, but, like cleaning a messy house, it feels better afterwards. If there is a lot of garbage, it won't all go in one sitting. It may take two or three sessions before you start enjoying life again.

Good meditators know the value of 'bad' meditations. They know it is good to 'just plod on', to 'do the scales', to 'clean up the garbage'. They also know what their minds are like. There is darkness within all of us. Even in the best circumstances, it is rare to get a series of beautiful meditations without at least some clouds across the sun.

What To Do when You Can't Focus at All

When you can't sustain your focus for more than a second or two, then there is little point in trying. It is time to practise detachment instead. If your mind is a dogfight, then don't try sort it out. Try to 'just watch' the dogfight instead. It may not be beautiful, but, as a spectator, at least you don't get bitten.

There is a simple reason why we can't we just 'get rid of' bad thoughts. We don't like them. If we react against a thought or sensation, we are giving it attention. We tense up and it still has its claws in us. We extract ourselves only when we 'just watch' it or accept its presence.

'Just watching', or awareness, seems a simple idea. In fact, it takes years to perfect. Some things, like a sore back or a loud car noise, are easy to notice and shrug off. Others, like extreme pain or an unresolvable conflict, are more difficult. Little by little, however, we realise we can 'just watch' anything at all.

'Just Watching' Develops Slowly

Detachment develops over time. Early in a course, if someone coughs during a meditation, I see faces and bodies tightening around the room. Other students are obviously irritated and feel they have to 'start again'. Yet, a few weeks later, a subtle change occurs. It often goes unnoticed at first. The 'distractions' are still there, but they have lost their claws and teeth. In fact, they are no longer distractions. People say things like:

'That car alarm startled me at first, but I soon got used to it.'
'My neck still aches, but I feel more relaxed anyway.'
'I struggled with thoughts for a little while, but they soon faded away.'

This detachment soon crops up outside of meditation:

'I was able to tell myself "Don't let it get at you" — and it didn't!'
'I no longer get so mad at the idiots on the road.'
'She tried to press my buttons, but I just stayed cool and watched her rave.'

We all have this ability to 'just watch'. It is there in every single moment of perception. When any thought or sensation arises in the mind, we first see it exactly as it is—the bare truth. It is just a car, or a jackhammer, or a man. A split second later, we get the emotional tone (which depends on our past associations with that object) and usually respond automatically: 'That's awful', 'That's nice', 'I don't like that,' and so on. The mind becomes busy, weaving thought and emotion around the original stimuli.

Perception is a two-stage process: first we see, then we respond. Meditation helps us create a pause between them, so our response is not so blind. By pausing to see clearly, we can respond consciously, or not at all, as we wish.

An old Indian text says the mind is like two birds in a tree. One bird eats the fruit (the mind that acts). The other just watches the first. Some part of us is always monitoring what we think and do. The bird that watches is always serene. After all, it doesn't have to do anything. It is also wise. It sees clearly, without desire or aversion.

The first bird is focused, even obsessed. It only sees the fruit. The second bird puts it in perspective. It also sees the trees, the sky, the clouds at sunset. The first bird sees a person and gets angry. The second bird sees the person, the anger, the tightening shoulders and the whole situation, with detachment.

Surprisingly, both minds can be present at once. A student once told me, 'I know exactly what you mean. I got furious once, which I very rarely do, and really let rip at someone. At the same time there was another me, behind my shoulder saying "Is that really you?"'

Both minds operate every second of the day. In meditation, you focus on the breath and explore it. That is the active mind doing something. The watching mind, however, monitors the rest — the passing parade of peripheral thoughts and sensations. Both minds are essential, but meditation particularly cultivates the watcher.

How To Meditate Amid Major Disturbances

If you are meditating and a door slams nearby, you could say 'Dammit!' and amplify your anger — 'Why can't people be more considerate!' Or you could just watch the process with detachment.

You hear the sound, and feel your body jerk. You can also 'just watch' your emotional response. You can't stop the flash of anger, but you can watch it pass. Perhaps you feel it within you as a hot flash, or a sudden prickling in the scalp. In time, you can watch this dissipate and feel the body settling. You may even feel pleased with yourself for remaining calm. This is yet another thought to 'just watch' without commentary.

If you are doing a classical awareness practice, you would 'name' all the stages: 'slamming door … anger … tensing up … annoyed at myself … releasing … breath softening … satisfaction …'

In the mini-drama above, it would be silly to try shutting out the sound and holding grimly to the breath. When a distraction is stronger than the meditation object, it is a good time to practise 'just watching'. It is often easier to return to the breath after you sense the distraction fully.

As we are all human, physical or emotional pain will always find us. We can't barricade ourselves against it permanently. Manning the barricades continuously will only keep us in a state of tension and fear, which is painful in itself.

We don't become tranquil by going to war and fighting against everything we don't like. Watching with detachment is a better strategy. It allows the moments of emotional pain to flare up and die a natural death. They are like showers of sparks from a fire. They usually peter out in seconds, unless we fan them into a blaze.

The emotional negativities — anger, despair, fear, attachment — burn when they arise. If we accept the momentary pain, they soon burn out. If we feed them or try to drive them away, however, they can smoulder for hours.

Some meditations are very challenging. If the mindstream is full of pain, then 'just watching' is a better strategy than focusing. You may name, in quick succession: 'sore neck ... frustration ... work ... itchy skin ... Lotto ... Roger ... headache ... miserable ... tonight's meal ... despair ... millennium bug... headache again ... sore stomach ... Iraq ... breathing ...'

The contents may not be attractive, but 'naming' tends to disarm them. You pull them off your back, one by one, and pigeonhole them. They often escape and return, but don't worry. Just pigeonhole them again. Soon you find you don't react so strongly to them. Some will fade, others will vanish altogether. You may still not be happy when you finish the meditation, but you will be more physically relaxed and less reactive than you were. This is progress. Congratulate yourself on a good meditation.

'Just watching' is the art of love and acceptance. The mind is not like a suitcase with a 20-kilogram weight restriction. It is vast enough to contain every thought, feeling, and experience from the past, present or future. Ultimately, meditation leads to a state of oneness. It is able to hold everything, without exception, in its embrace — even the barking dog, even the slamming door.

The secret is to let go the good, and not resist the bad. If we can let everything come and go, nothing will stick in the mind unless we want it to. We can be fearless. No thought will ever be a threat or temptation. We can have serenity in the midst of chaos. Thich Nhat Hanh, the contemporary Zen master, describes this state as being 'on the lotus in the sea of fire'.

SPOT MEDITATION: WATCHING THE CHAOS

If your day has been pure hell and any attempt to discipline the mind seems like masochism, then try this exercise. Don't try to focus. Just practise detachment. Open the cages of the mind and let the savage beasts run riot.

Instructions

- Let go. Give up all effort except the effort to let go.
- Don't try to sit correctly or focus on one thing.
- Let the wild animals run — problems, pain, fantasy, fears, anger. Stand back and watch them. Resist the compulsion to run after them, picking up their droppings.
- Every few seconds, ask yourself: 'What's going on now?', then name the strongest thought or sensation. Don't try to fix anything — just take an inventory of the mess. If several things are bugging you, rotate through them in turn so you don't get stuck on any one of them.
- Enjoy the relief of complete despair. Tell yourself you are incapable of productive thought at this moment. It's probably true, so do nothing. Be like an irresponsible parent who couldn't care less about his or her kids. Let them sort themselves out.
- Notice when you are thinking about something. Name it. Throw it away. Wait for the next thought or sensation and name that, too.

CHAPTER 12

Meditating for Better Health

I receive several phone calls a week from people who say, 'My doctor said I should learn to meditate.' About a quarter of my students are referred to me by their general practitioners. People instinctively *feel* that stress is bad for health and feel that meditation can help. The doctors, however, *know* meditation is valuable because they have read the literature.

Doctors are on firm ground when they tell patients that meditation can help their health. They are backed up by hundreds, perhaps thousands, of scientific studies over many years. The jury has delivered its verdict. Meditation is not a quack remedy. If you are sick, meditation can help you heal. If you are not sick, meditation will help to keep you healthy.

Some meditation groups claim that meditation is universally good for everything — the scientific evidence doesn't go that far yet. It does show, however, that meditation has specific effects and that it works better in some cases than in others. At the very least, it generally does no harm to meditate. The only obvious contraindications are in cases of schizophrenia.

The main reason meditation helps is because you are able to relax quickly and more deeply than you would otherwise. In other words, most of its benefits are the same as those of deep relaxation — you just get more of it than you usually would. Meditators know there are further benefits. Although these are not yet corroborated by research, they make sense psychologically. I talk about them more in chapter 18, 'Emotional healing', on pages 131–143.

Meditation Stimulates the Immune System

The immune system combats disease and helps the body repair itself. When we are tense, however, or mentally active, we produce cortisol and adrenaline. These are immunosuppressants. They suppress the self-healing mechanism of the body. When we are tense and anxious, all resources are directed to the outer emergency and the immune system function shuts down. In other words, the body is able to repair itself only in those minutes or hours when we are relaxed or asleep.

In brief, when you are anxious, you switch the immune system off; when you relax, you switch it on. If you are sick, it is best to relax, even amid the pain, and do very little. This is the principle of convalescence. It is even better if the mind is relaxed—in alpha rather than beta mode. I am sure this is why studies show that meditation speeds recovery rates after surgery or illness.

Meditation Releases Muscular Tension and Pain

When tense, the muscles become rigid and hard. Tense shoulders, for example, burn a lot of kilojoules to stay hard. Tension is exhausting— it drains our energy reserves.

Many of us put on a happy face, but we have our own 'Gulag Archipelago' inside. We can have little pockets of extreme tension around the body, like concentration camps, hidden out of sight and mind. These can be small, but deadly places. Chronically tight muscles will quite literally die, in time, from malfunction caused by stress.

A rigid body carries more pain throughout. Bone and muscle seem to grate against each other. Apart from obvious pain, there can be much 'micro' pain through the body — parts that are numb and a little sore, rather than obviously painful.

Tense muscles, moreover, are more likely to tear when used. If we hurt ourselves, the adjacent muscles often tense up around the injury to provide a kind of splint. Unfortunately, this makes them vulnerable to damage themselves. They are less able to stretch when a load is put on them. When we relax, however, the muscles become softer and more supple. They burn less energy, so the body operates more economically. We don't get so tired, and we can do more for longer.

Relaxed muscles expand and contract gracefully, without the jerkiness of a habitually tense body. This makes them less subject to the many little injuries that occur when the body is rigid. A supple body has less 'micro' pain and feels more comfortable to inhabit. Without quite knowing why, we just feel better and the day is more enjoyable.

Meditation Lowers High Blood Pressure

The release in muscular tension makes the body more pliable. The blood also becomes thinner as we relax, as the cholesterol drains away. This combination of a more supple body and thinner blood means the heart doesn't have to pump so hard to force the blood through the veins and arteries. So the pressure comes down.

There are thousands of muscles in the body. I think hypertension declines because, if you meditate, those muscles are all just a little more relaxed all the time. For this reason, I find that hypertension in new meditators usually takes about a month to decline. It takes people that long to reset their general tension levels. Hypertension often declines dramatically, however, and stays down.

Meditation Improves Blood Circulation and Body Function

When tense, the blood becomes thick with cholesterol (a source of quick-release energy). The fight-or-flight mechanism diverts the blood to the big internal muscles, ready for action. The blood, however, has to come from somewhere. It drains away from the skin, the brain and the digestive tract. The mind is saying, 'There's an emergency here. I won't waste time digesting food.'

Tight muscles cramp the breathing. They impede the flow of blood through the veins, arteries and capillaries. They impinge on nerve fibres and shut off the signals. They clamp down on the ebb and flow rhythms of peristalsis. I imagine they inhibit the proper secretion of hormones and juices from their appropriate organs.

When we relax, the muscles soften. The blood thins out and flows freely again. People often feel this as a pleasant tingling or warmth on the skin. People occasionally report: 'My hands and feet are always cold, except when I meditate!'

A good blood flow is very healthy for the organs involved. The cells are well supplied with nutrients and waste products are removed efficiently. Conversely, when the body is tense, the city gates are closed. Few supplies come in and the waste isn't removed. Being tense means you starve the cells and poison them in their own excreta.

Despite our admiration for 'hard bodies', a healthy body is actually supple, soft and fluid. I massaged a body-builder once. His muscles were like jelly. They looked and were strong because they could relax so totally. This is the yin and yang of the body. If you want to be strong, then learn to be soft. If you want energy, then learn to be still.

Being healthy is not about reading the right books and eating the right food. It is about recognising the feeling of flow and good health in the body. To put it simply, all you need to do is notice your subtle physical (and emotional) tensions, and relax into them. If you practise the body-scan meditation, you can take this right down to the micro level. It is like combing the knots out of your energy field and restoring that effervescent, childlike feeling of flow and life within you.

Meditation Balances Brain Activity

Meditation balances the activities of the left and right hemispheres of the brain. This is easy to see on an electro-encephalograph. The left hemisphere governs the motor coordination of the right side of the body, and vice versa. If these hemispheres are not coordinated, the body is lopsided, unbalanced and doesn't move harmoniously.

People who are tense tie themselves in knots. They unconsciously cross their arms and legs tightly, and sit awkwardly slouched or twisted in a chair.

As they relax, the hemispheres balance and they sit more openly. This conserves energy, relieves pain and enables them to breathe freely.

The hemispheres also govern mental functions. To put it crudely, the right hemisphere usually controls sensing and feeling, the left controls thinking and analysing. The right sees connections; the left makes distinctions.

Our thinking and feeling functions are often out of balance, or even at odds with each other. Some people are awash with feeling and can't think straight. Others are so caught in their word-chatter they lose touch with their non-verbal feelings. Meditators, however, get the best of both worlds. They balance on the bridge between the two, able to think rationally and feel deeply at the same time.

The two hemispheres are connected by a thick bridge of nerve fibres called the *corpus callosum*. Women (and left-handed people) tend to have thicker bridges than men, indicating greater communication between thinking and feeling functions. You could say that meditation strengthens the intuitive and female qualities of men. Women possibly learn to think clearer.

Meditation Seems To Retard Ageing

As we get older, our hormones adjust to cope with an ageing body. A meditator's pattern of hormonal secretions is often typical of someone five or ten years younger than themselves. This suggests that the physical stresses of age do not weigh so heavily on a meditator. This is why some groups promote meditation as a beauty treatment. 'You can eliminate those wrinkles and take five years off your looks.' This is not just a hard sell. There is some evidence to suggest this is true. Meditators often look younger than their actual age.

Some people age quickly, some age slowly. An alcoholic can be an old man at forty. People who stay fit often have the bodies of much younger people. Meditators likewise, carry their years well, inwardly and outwardly.

I think the reasons are obvious. Meditators stay healthy and enjoy life. That is a big plus. Evidence shows that meditators have very low rates of serious illness or hospital admissions.

In Europe, some insurance companies even give meditators discounts on their health policies for this reason.

Meditation Is Good for Certain Ailments

People often come to my classes for a specific ailment. Meditation has an excellent track record in the treatment of migraines, insomnia, hypertension, chronic pain, asthma, allergies and recovery from illness. It is also good for psychosomatic disorders of the skin, digestive tract and the nervous system.

With insomnia and migraines, meditation sometimes acts like a magic bullet. I once had a bank manager at my classes. He had suffered migraines one or twice a week for thirty years. By the second week, they were completely gone. Nonetheless, he attended another course, just to make sure. Years have passed, but I still see him in the street. 'No migraines' he reports, 'as long as I meditate!' I have seen many other migraine sufferers respond almost as well.

Insomniacs also respond well to meditation. It seems to strip off the top 20 per cent of physical tension that triggers insomnia or a migraine attack. In general, people sleep well in the night after a meditation class. Sometimes I see complete joy on a person's face when they report: 'Last night I slept for six hours without a break!' Other insomniacs find meditation helps them go back to sleep when they wake at night.

The effects of meditation on hypertension are obvious. There is nothing subjective about it. It is all about numbers. And the numbers come down. High blood pressure usually comes down fairly slowly. It is as if the person is adjusting to a new way of being—but it can come down a long way and stay down. Some people actually feel their blood pressure falling as they meditate. It tends to stay down for a few hours after the meditation is over.

Meditation is particularly good for asthmatics and hay-fever sufferers. The research says that meditation opens constricted air passages. I once had a woman on a retreat who had forgotten her inhaler. She normally needed twenty-odd puffs a day. She relaxed so well she got through the whole weekend without it.

People in severe pain often find immediate relief. Such people are among my best students. They know meditation works, and they practise well. Some have managed to avoid operations as their pain becomes more manageable.

People with serious digestive problems often find meditation helps. The reason is quite obvious. When we are tense, the digestive system shuts down. The body's energy is going elsewhere. We only digest food well when we are relaxed. If we never relax well, the system never works well. One of my students was able to avoid bowel surgery just by taking up meditation.

Women trying to fall pregnant often succeed when they learn to meditate. Presumably, a relaxed body creates a better environment for conception. Women who have suffered miscarriages in the past often find they can carry their babies to term. It feels strange to know that, by teaching their mothers, I am indirectly responsible for the successful birth of many children around Perth. (As far as I know, none of them have yet been named after me!)

People taking pills for psychosomatic complaints often find they can reduce their dosages. People commonly learn meditation to get off their pills, and they often succeed. Smokers who want to quit often find meditation helps.

Meditation works well for some psychological disorders. People who suffer panic attacks, or who have obsessive–compulsive disorders, find they cope much better. The usual behavioural techniques taught to such people are very similar to meditation. Although the complaint rarely disappears completely, it becomes just a minor irritant.

Meditation has ambivalent results with depression. This is because of the way people use the practice. Meditation can clarify the mind fog, so you see more accurately what is happening. This helps people understand the patterns and triggers, so they can eventually extract themselves.

Other depressed people, however, can use meditation to pull the bed-covers over their heads. They relax, but fog out. They can stay there a long time, peaceful but lost. This may still be better than so-called 'agitated depression' which carries high anxiety with it. Meditation in this case at least gives the body a break from thought and a chance to rest.

Meditation and Serious Illness

Many people who attend my classes have cancer, are recovering from a cancer operation or are holding it at bay. Sometimes people say to me things like: 'I believe meditation can cure cancer.' I prefer to say that meditation supports a cure, rather than causes it. Even doctors don't 'cure' anything. They only assist the natural healing processes of the body.

As support, meditation may be vital for a cure. If we don't stake up a young tree, for example, it may be blown over and die. The support, however, would be only one of many factors in producing a healthy tree. Meditation may be the crucial factor that helps a person overcome cancer, but it is unlikely to be the sole cause. Lifestyle, diet, medical intervention and psychological factors will all play a part.

Serious illnesses are complex. Cancer, perhaps because of its sudden onset, often propels people into examining their life, changing priorities and living according to new schedules and demands.

In this context, meditation can be very valuable. People meditate to cope with the discomfort of treatment, to manage the changing dynamics in their life, to see their inner turmoil more clearly, to help them be more reflective and thoughtful. They can also do quite specific meditations for physical and mental healing. (See chapter 18 on emotional healing on pages 131–143.)

Summary

There is no doubt that meditation is good for your health. The scientific evidence is clear, and doctors are often happy to recommend meditation to their patients. It is good to remember, however, that some people take this to a superstitious extreme.

Christian Science and New Age belief argues that a healthy mind creates a healthy body. Consequently, ruddy, good health is seen as a clear sign of spiritual accomplishment, and vice versa. (This belief can also be seen in the way certain sports stars get the adulation afforded to gods.) Some people, in ancient China and modern California, feel that if you perfect your mind, you will never die.

I don't think it is that simple. You often find very healthy minds in decaying bodies. In fact, some of the greatest meditation teachers of the nineteenth and twentieth centuries have succumbed to illnesses such as cancer at a relatively early age. Our health is such an emotional issue. Most of us struggle with it to some degree. Rather than adopt irrational beliefs about the powers of the mind, I think it is better to stick close to the facts.

Sometimes meditation acts like a magic bullet. Generally it works more like naturopathic treatment: it brings the whole body into balance. The results are slower, more pervasive and not so easy to measure.

If you meditate, you are likely to sleep better, digest your food better, breathe better, move gracefully and have more energy. Your immune system will function better and your blood pressure should be close to normal. You will suffer less from anxiety-induced disorders, have less physical pain and tension, be more relaxed and mentally clear, and enjoy life more. By managing your body in this way, you give it a much better chance to cope with any illness you may have.

MEDITATION: WHITE LIGHT

This is the the body scan meditation of chapter 6 (page 51) augmented with imagery and feeling. You scan the body from top to bottom, imagining light, water or nectar flowing through all the flesh, bones and organs, right down to the cellular level. It is usual to say a mantra such as 'Om mani peme hung', or an appropriate affirmation, as you do it.

When tense or sick, we often grimly try to fight the illness. This is not healthy. The body often contracts into itself like a fortress. This visualisation does the reverse. Instead of being tense and fighting, you evoke a passive and receptive state of mind. You imagine the body being hollow, 'like a tent made of white silk', and the healing energy of the universe flowing into you from above.

Some people imagine it as light, illuminating and dissolving the blockages. Others feel it as sparkling spring water, washing things clean. Others sense it as nectar or mother's milk, nourishing the hurt body. Others feel it as divine love, or as the breath of life.

This meditation has many possibilities. Often it is best for the light to be soft and soothing at first, like moonlight. Later, however, it may become bright and crystal-like. This can ferret out and illuminate all the gunk and rubbish within you. Often this needs to be seen and felt clearly before it shakes loose and washes out.

Don't worry if you can't seem to visualise. Just pretend that you can. The feeling is actually more important than the imagery. Be playful

MEDITATION: WHITE LIGHT (continued)

and childlike, and don't try too hard. Many people find it easier to 'feel' rather than 'see'. If you are like this, then imagine stroking, massaging or caressing the body instead.

This meditation works best if it is not just a picture show. It is good to feel each part of the body in detail, as in the body-scan meditation, while also playing with the images.

Instructions

- Relax the body and breathing for a minute.
- Now, imagine the body is empty 'like a tent made of white silk'. It is hollow, but still full of sensations. Some are heavy and dense. Some are light and subtle. Imagine your breath to be a gentle breeze, caressing your energy field from the feet to the crown of the head and back again.
- Imagine the crown of the head opening, like a white flower in full bloom. When you feel completely open, imagine light, water, space or nectar (or any combination) from the sky above, flowing into your body. Say a mantra or affirmation if you wish.
- Feel the light flow through the scalp, down the face, behind the eyes, into the brain, and so on. Slowly and deliberately, for the bulk of the meditation, feel the light going through every part of your body — illuminating, nourishing, washing the rubbish free.
- Eventually feel your whole body is glowing. It may feel more tactile than visual, like the hum of life within you. Imagine your body surrounded by a cocoon or bubble of light.
- Feel the light that was above you now radiating from your heart through your entire body and beyond. Rest in that light or that inner feeling as long as you wish.
- Eventually let the light shrink and dissolve within you, like a star fading into inner space. Know it is always there, but come back to your everyday body. Finally, rest with the breath. Notice if you are fully relaxed, or if you were trying too hard.

CHAPTER 13

Being in Touch
with Reality

People sometimes wonder if meditation is an escape from reality. Certainly, when we relax, the world seems different. Meditation can change your outlook, but even positive changes can be disconcerting. If you find yourself calm in a crisis, you may wonder: 'Am I becoming cold-hearted and unfeeling?'

If to 'be in touch with reality' is to worry about things that haven't happened, fret over things that can't be changed and react with panic to daily events, then the answer is 'yes'. Meditation is an escape from all of that.

A person who is chronically tense will see the world through the beta-brainwave state of mind. This is the reality of money, work, superannuation, getting the kids through school and the Gross National Product. It is fuelled by fear, anger and desire. We can live entirely in this state if we want. We could call this 'male' reality.

A person who is able to relax, however, sees the world differently. From the alpha state, the concerns of the future and past vanish. We are more alive to sensation and feeling, more in touch with our bodies and the present moment. We feel safe where we are and don't want anything we haven't got. We could regard this as a more 'female' reality. When we stroke a cat or enjoy an apple, are we really 'out of touch with reality'?

When we fall asleep, we enter yet another reality. Dreams are real to us when we are in them. Are dreams a complete illusion just because they don't match waking reality? So which perspective is real? The beta or the alpha or the dream perspective? Is one more real, or more important, than the others?

Meditation enhances alpha reality. This can be disturbing for people who operate on high adrenalin levels. They can't imagine being relaxed while awake. It is as if their bodies only have an on/off switch, and relaxing can only mean sleep and oblivion. They may even believe it is dangerous to relax. Perhaps it will turn you into a zombie or drive you insane. For a few years, I received anonymous Christian tracts through the mail warning me of the dangers. Some people regard me as doing very evil work.

Yet the concern of some is genuine. 'If I go into meditation, I may not want to come back. Who would pick up the kids after school?' When you relax, you experience yourself as you really are. You may find you are exhausted — and have been exhausted for years. Behind the smiling mask, you may find deep anger or sadness. When Christians say 'the devil leaps into an empty mind', they have a point. Except that the devil is often a hidden part of you.

Using Meditation as Escapism

Of course, you can use meditation to escape, if you want to. People often turn to a spiritual path to avoid facing their problems. When people can relax deeply, they often resent the outer world. They feel that the demands of children, work and life itself are undermining their spirituality. *If only I could meditate all day*, they think. *If only I could go to India or be with the teacher continuously, or lead the pure life, I could really progress inwardly.*

Unfortunately, this antagonism towards ordinary life is encouraged by many religious groups in the East and West. Cults, in particular, encourage an infantile dependency amongst their followers, and demonise the world beyond the fence.

At the micro level of a single meditation session, some people also try to escape. Although meditation is an alert state, as you relax deeply, it becomes harder to stay sharp. Some people enjoy this lack of clarity, and become practised at sitting in a torpor. They don't quite fall off the chair, but they are not very awake. It is actually a calm state, which is why they enjoy it, but anaesthetised and rather dull as well.

Some meditators get stuck in the state for years. They say things like 'I can switch my mind off whenever I want to.' This is called 'dead-stump' or 'bronze-Buddha' practice. They look good, but nothing is happening. It is like a self-induced Valium doze.

The assumption that meditation is somehow a blanked-out state goes very deep. Even good meditators can have a sneaking fondness for oblivion—and try to achieve it. They enjoy the cloudiness and indulge the fantasies that arise.

It is not a bad thing to do occasionally. It is quite healthy to be this relaxed. The quality is poor, however, and it will never go far. Unless there is more clarity, there is no hope of enjoying the full fruits of meditation.

Meditating with the Eyes Open

Meditation keeps you in touch with reality only if you choose to remain alert. An excellent way to stay awake is to meditate with your eyes open. I like to train people to at least start and finish a meditation with their eyes open. It is easier if they keep their eyes soft, or almost out of focus. Their eyes should be resting on something in front of them—a spot on the carpet will do—to resist the temptation to scan the room.

Many people find this idea absurd at first. They say things like: 'As soon as I opened my eyes, it was all over.' Often they feel pleasantly fuzzy with their eyes closed. Opening their eyes, however, shocks them out of this pleasant torpor.

Others want to know why they should be able to meditate with open eyes. 'It's so much easier with my eyes closed,' they complain. There is a very long list of reasons why.

You can meditate anywhere and anytime — in queues, in boring meetings, in lectures, while walking or doing exercise or housework. You can voluntarily take time out and cool down your mind. And no one notices. If you have to keep your eyes closed, your meditation is very limited. It remains something you can only do in private, like getting undressed.

If you are struggling to stay awake in a meditation, you can open your eyes. This will automatically make you more awake.

You can meditate on things of beauty. A rose, a candle flame, a crystal— these are classical meditation objects. You can also focus on a tree, clouds, the wind in the grass, the colours of sunset, a bird in the scrub, sunlight sparkling off water, a dead leaf, a spider web, the night sky.

People often get bored, meditating all their life on the breath or a mantra. They don't realise that the ability to focus is much more important than the object, and they can easily shift their focus to something else. It is easy to meditate on something we find enchanting.

Meditating on outer things deepens our sense-pleasure and empathy with nature. It counteracts the introspective 'navel-gazing' tendency into which meditators can fall. We realise we can actually use the outer world to meditate. We don't have to shut it out and escape inside in order to relax.

We see more deeply into things. We pick up fine detail. People often say with delight things like: 'I don't think I've ever looked so deeply before at a rose [crystal, flame, driftwood, apple, blade of grass ...'

A clear mind is not empty. It is a mind that sees clearly. It is like having clean spectacles. You can see accurately, in full detail, whatever is before you. If your meditation is foggy, that fogginess can last after the meditation is over. Conversely, if your meditation is clear, that clarity continues afterwards. People say things like:

> 'When I come in here after work, I never notice the park. But when I leave, the trees all look so alive and beautiful.'
> 'I always study better after meditating.'
> 'After I meditate, everything is heightened. It's almost too intense.'
> 'For the first time, I understood what was happening between me and my daughter.'

Meditation changes peoples lives for the better. This is not just because we relax more and sleep better. It is because the mind is clearer. We wake up and see what is happening. We are in touch, from moment to moment, with the physical sensations and emotions of being alive. For better or worse, we are in touch with reality.

SPOT MEDITATION: VISUAL OBJECT

Most people do this meditation casually. They find themselves with a moment to spare, so they focus on something in front of them. Conversely, when something catches their attention, they deliberately let other thoughts go and focus on it.

I usually teach this meditation by putting several objects on a table — a vase of flowers, a candle, a mango, a piece of driftwood, a silk scarf. Some students are interested in none of these, and focus on the carpet instead.

We can look at the object photographically, as it were, in terms of colour and form. Or thoughts and memories may arise around the object. You may realise that your grandmother had those flowers in her backyard, for example, or you may find yourself imagining the taste, texture and insides of the mango.

When I was a child, I used to imagine what an ant would see as it climbed through a tree. If you wish, you can let your imagination play. You can go inside an object or imagine climbing a crystal as if was a mountain. Meditation should have at least a smidgen of childlike play about it.

The instructions below are fairly loose. Your mind may be fairly active or calm. You may be using your imagination or seeing the object plain. You may be 'naming' the object or not. There are many possibilities and you may wonder if you are 'doing it right'. To check, you can ask yourself:

• Am I with the object?

SPOT MEDITATION: VISUAL OBJECT (continued)

- Am I sensing more than thinking?
- Am I in the present?
- Is my body relaxing?
- Do I feel better afterwards?

Instructions

- Let your eyes settle on something in front of you. Let the eye muscles be loose. They can be almost out of focus. Nonetheless, first spend a few seconds letting your body and breath settle down.
- Explore the object gently and slowly. Don't stare. It is like stroking or touching the object with your gaze. Take the object in. Savour it. Notice colour, shape, texture, shadow patterns, and so on.
- If you wish, 'name' the object each time you breathe out. Or you can name the colour, if you find that attractive. Or you can name both colour and object: 'red [as you breathe in] … daisy [as you breathe out]'. Naming is not essential, but it can help.
- Explore the object in your imagination, if you wish, but don't be too active, or 'creative'. Just play along with what arises naturally. When the mind wanders off, 'name' the distraction and return to your object.
- Close your eyes, if you wish, and go over the memory of the object in your mind. The image may change somewhat. Naming usually helps.
- Periodically check your body to make sure you are actually relaxing.

CHAPTER 14

Walking Meditations

People often walk to relax. A dawn stroll by the river or a ramble round the back streets or a local park may be your way of relaxing. Walking takes you into no-man's-land, away from home, work and responsibilities. You can't do anything but walk and think. You are alone with your thoughts. Walking puts you in touch with yourself and nature.

You are actually following in the footsteps of the Indian holy men of old. The students of the Buddha were not monks. That came later. They were 'wanderers' or 'homeless ones', who brushed the dust of city life from their feet and roamed. Like full-time pilgrims, they wandered all their lives.

Walking is as ancient a meditation posture as sitting. Australian Aborigines go 'walkabout'. Native Americans go on a spirit quest. Young men and women of all times leave the cozy certainties of home to find themselves. Walking reminds us of our nomadic ancestry when we owned nothing and faced each day afresh.

'Leave your homeland to awaken,' said the Buddha. His students were encouraged to spend no more than three days in one place (except during the rainy season). So they walked a lot and, in time, developed walking into a deliberate meditation practice.

The original holy men and women went naked or wore cast-off rags. Nowadays, the monks often dress very well, in pressed robes of silk and brocade. Similarly, over 2500 years, the walking meditations that were once very simple have become elaborate and formal.

Zen practitioners may walk in a circle, synchronising their steps. A Burmese monk may walk extremely slowly, verbally noting each micro-movement of his feet. (This is not very relaxing, but it makes the mind extremely sharp and alert.) Kung Fu and Tai Chi are developments of the Buddhist and Taoist standing and walking meditations.

On retreats, people often alternate sitting and walking meditations. These complement each other well. It is usual to walk slowly backwards and forwards on a strip of ground about 20 metres long, with eyes looking downwards. Sitting makes you calm, but a little dull. Walking wakes you up, but is not so relaxing. After a sitting meditation, you walk to wake up. After a walking meditation, you sit to settle down.

Yet ordinary walking, like ordinary breathing, is still the best. It means you can meditate any time you are moving—walking down the hall, to the shops, through the park, in a crowded street. You can put thoughts on hold, drop into the present and enjoy the sensations of just being alive.

Softening the Eyes

Obviously, while walking, you also notice other people, kerbs, cars, trees, sky and birds. The trick is to keep them in the periphery of the mind. Usually, because they are sensations of the present, they are less distracting than thoughts anyway. Nonetheless, it is good to sedate your eyes somewhat.

Our eyes usually hop from attraction to attraction like summer flies. Wherever the eyes go, the mind follows. When we are anxious, the little muscles that swivel the eyeballs can be quite active.

There are three things you can do with your eyes. First, you can hook them, like casting a fishing line, over a point in the distance—a tree or car—and reel yourself in towards it. This helps you resist glancing sideways. Secondly, you can look down at the ground, 3 or 4 metres ahead. You can see where you are going, but not much else. This also makes you look serious and pious. Finally, you can just let your eyes glaze slightly, so they rest back in their sockets. Try to evoke the way your eyes feel when you emerge from a sitting meditation—soft and gentle, and maybe even a little out of focus.

In any of the above strategies, your peripheral vision will still be active enough to stop you bumping into strangers and falling over kerbs. Here are some possible walking meditations:

MEDITATION ONE: WALKING COMFORTABLY

An old Buddhist aphorism goes 'when walking, just walk'. In other words, enjoy the sensations of the body moving, but don't get lost in thought as well. If you sense your body move, you will soon find yourself walking more comfortably. Walking is a posture like any other. The same guidelines apply — comfort, balance and alertness. We aim to walk comfortably with no excess tension. The body should be straight and balanced, to allow free movement. It often helps to scan the body up and down as you walk.

If we are anxious, we walk anxiously. You can see it any city street. People walk with a stiff gait, hunched shoulders, tight breathing and staring eyes. Their anxieties are mirrored in their gait.

The body enjoys moving. Walking can be a lovely, rhythmic movement. Parents use it to soothe their babies. Walking is healthy and feels good. It moves the juices along, and keeps muscles and brain alive. If we are too sedentary, both body and mind become sluggish and dull. If we don't move enough, the muscles atrophy. If we stop moving altogether, parts of the body start dying — and that doesn't feel good at all.

Walking is rhythmic, and anything rhythmic soothes the mind. Often the body processes start to synchronise. You breathe in time with the foot-steps. The shoulders and hips swing easily. The continuous ripple of sensation massage the muscles made tight by too much sitting or thinking.

When meditating on walking, the same principles apply as for any other meditation. You put a 'fence' around your body and explore it. When you notice your mind has jumped the fence, you 'name' the distraction and return to the body.

MEDITATION TWO: COUNTING THE STEPS

We may often want to do a walking meditation when the mind is very scattered. In this case, you give it something crude and obvious upon which to focus. You count your footsteps. This meditation seems rather silly, but it works well for many people. It is a good emergency practice.

As we can all count automatically, we need to make the counting more complex. So, we count from one to five steps, then from one to six, then to seven, then to eight. And then back to one to five, and so on. We just walk at our natural speed, and count the steps: '1, 2, 3, 4, 5, 1, 2, 3, 4, 5, 6, 1, 2, 3, 4, 5, 6, 7 ...', and so on.

You find that anything that brings you into the present, such as counting steps, also makes you more aware of other things in the present.

By counting, you extract yourself from thought. Soon you find yourself enjoying the sights, sounds and smells around you as well.

MEDITATION THREE: THE BREATH

You are aware of both breathing and walking at once in this meditation practice. Runners often synchronise their breathing with their legs. They may take four steps as they breathe in and four as they breathe out, for example. In this meditation, you notice roughly how many steps you take on the in-breath and how many on the out-breath. Then you synchronise them, and count the steps. You may walk to a '3 ... 4 ...', or a '4 ... 4 ...', or a '5 ... 6 ...'. Usually the out-breath is longer than the in-breath. If the breath wants to change, then just adjust the pattern.

MEDITATION FOUR: RANDOM SOUND

The meditations above all focus inwardly on the body and the breath. This is a good way to start any walking meditation. You could also, however, focus outwardly. There are many ways to go about this. It is still good to be disciplined. If you let the mind wander at random, the meditation will soon dissolve into a 'nothing-much' state.

So, you could make sounds your meditation object. Though you notice many sensations while walking, you deliberately highlight the sounds. You actively savour each sound that catches your attention, and move consciously from one sound to the next.

MEDITATION FIVE: WIND

This is a very ancient practice. You sense the wind coming and going against your skin. Even on a still day, the air masses shift around you — touching your cheek, leg or neck. This is a very sensual practice. It is like feeling the earth breathing over you. This is also a good practice if you are just sitting outside.

MEDITATION SIX: VISUAL OBJECT

Your mind can easily become scattered if you just go out and look at things. The mind needs to stay with something for at least eight seconds before it starts to slow down. If you skip from thing to thing, it speeds up again. I suggest you focus inwards on your breath or body, to give you a stable base. When something catches your eye, go out and enjoy it fully. When you walk past it, or let it go, however, you should return to the body rather than skip on to something else. So, your attention goes in and out, from the body to an object, then back to the body and out again.

MEDITATION SEVEN: SNAPSHOT

In this meditation, you take a snapshot. You give total attention to something for a short period of time. You aim for a few seconds of intense focus, rather than the averaged-out awareness we usually have. You drop all other thoughts and become totally absorbed in a leaf, a bird's feather, bark on a tree or a shadow on a wall, for instance. You imprint it in the mind. The 'exposure' may be for one second or twenty seconds.

As you walk on, play over the snapshot in your mind. We can take in a surprising amount of detail in just a few seconds. At the end of the day, you should be able to recall your snapshots and enjoy them again. I can remember snapshots from years ago.

Snapshots are a good training ground for visualisation. Many people are unable to imagine a rose, for example, because they haven't consciously looked at one for years. We first have to see something fully before it goes into the memory bank for later recall.

MEDITATION EIGHT: SENSING

In this meditation, you focus on whatever arises through any of the senses as you walk. So what makes this different from an ordinary stroll in the park? You don't skim. You sink into the detail of each thing and hold it for at least eight seconds. You savour the smell of the earth, the sight of birds fighting, a blast of wind at your ear, the crunch of bark and leaves underfoot as each enters the mind. You know exactly what you are focused on in that moment — and don't drift away in the spaces in between.

MEDITATIONS NINE AND TEN: SPACE AND LIGHT

Say the word 'space' as you take in the feeling of the sky above you. Internalise it. Imagine breathing the space into your body. Alternatively, you can focus on light. Notice the quality of light everywhere. Don't focus on the trees themselves, but on the light glittering through them. Don't focus on the building, but on the light shining off it. Internalise the light, so you feel yourself shining from within.

MEDITATION ELEVEN: WALKING PEACEFULLY

Say the world 'peace' as you walk. Feel in harmony with yourself and the world. Let your footsteps fall gently on the earth, and feel the earth respond. You could also use any other appropriate mantra or affirmation.

Walking meditations, like listening to music, are easy and pleasant. This can be a problem. Because you feel good, and there are many distractions anyway, your discipline gets poor and you let the mind drift. Soon you are just walking in the park, with your usual mix of thoughts and sensations.

In these meditations, the mind often shifts from one sensation to another. The secret is to shift slowly. Learn to linger on each thing. Your body may be moving quickly, but your mind should be slow and reflective. Remember that the mind needs at least eight seconds of focus to start shifting from beta to alpha brainwaves. Less focus than that and the mind starts speeding up and unravelling.

It is good to be systematic. It is best to practise a single meditation at least four times over four days. This takes you beyond the initial awkwardness and engraves the practice in long-term memory.

CHAPTER 15

Visualisation

An image is just like any other meditation object. You focus on it and explore it. When the mind wanders to something else, you 'name' the distraction and return to the image. If you focus well and are not too mentally active around the image, you will relax just as deeply as with the breath or a mantra.

Some people visualise easily. They may find the breath boring to watch, but they can readily imagine their child's face, a rose, a rainbow or a scene in the country. For them, focusing on something imaginary can be easier than focusing on something real.

Yet we can all visualise. This is how memory works. Try it out right now. Can you imagine an apple? What kind is it? Red Delicious, Granny Smith? Big or small? Feel its texture and weight in your hand. Is it smooth or waxy or slightly sticky? Imagine biting into it. Feel the resistance of the skin before it breaks. Is it crisp or a little soft? Notice the first burst of smell and taste. Hear the sound as you bite off a piece, and feel it in your mouth. Imagine swallowing it.

This exercise probably evoked something in you — a passing image, memory or sensation at least. Maybe you started salivating. You may not have had a clear visual picture, but you are probably more sensually aware of apples than before.

'Visualisation' is an unsatisfactory word. The above exercise evoked all five senses, not just sight. A better term would be *sensualisation*. Silva, the grandfather of American mind-training teachers, suggests you project an image onto a mental screen in front of you. I find only about 20 per cent of people can do this easily.

Not everyone is so visually orientated. Others can more readily evoke sound, touch, smell or taste. How did you go with the apple? Which was the clearest sensation?

Most people can evoke a feeling or mood. They are *kinesthetic* visualisers. Mood and feeling is stronger for them than visual pictures, which tend to fade quickly. You are visualising well when your body responds as if the object is actually present.

Read the following sequence slowly. Give the image and mood a few seconds to arise. Linger on the images that grab you. Notice if your body responds. It may expand, tighten or recoil, for example. Notice any accompanying emotion. Can you evoke the feeling of any of the following?:

- being in bed with your partner (or teddy bear);
- a melting ice-cream cone;
- intense pain;
- an open fire;
- the smell of petrol;
- a flowering bush;
- a baby's skin;
- a dead animal on the road;
- being at the beach;
- your grandmother.

I am sure some images caught your attention more than others. Some images may have arisen spontaneously, without any effort on your part.

A good visualisation works on three dimensions. These are imagery, emotion and body response. The first is obvious. It is an image involving one or more of the senses.

The second is an accompanying emotion that fits just this image and no other. You may love both your children, but your feeling towards each one will be unique. An image that evokes this subtlety of feeling will hold your attention better than a mere picture.

The third level is body response. This is when the body responds as if you are actually there! If you imagine being under a cold shower, your body will start to contract. If you imagine basking in the sun, it will start to expand.

If you are visualising for healing, evoking images alone is too superficial. A clear image, in fact, is less important than the feeling and the body response.

Where Do I Want To Be?

By visualising, we can give ourselves a holiday on the spot. We don't have to wait till Christmas. We can go the beach or to the country in our minds. I like to tailor these escapist fantasies to my exact mood. I ask: 'Where would I like to be, right now?' and wait for the images to arise.

They are often quite precise, and different each time. Perhaps I want to be sitting under the hanging branches of a tree, at dusk in autumn, with mist around the hills. Maybe I want to be in the Arctic tundra in midsummer, or perhaps with my friend in New Zealand, having a cup of tea on the verandah.

In a good visualisation, each detail is like a holograph and contains the emotion of the whole. It is better to go deeply into single details than attempt to paint an entire picture. Imagine the steam swirling from the cup of tea, the smell of the earth, the sounds of distant birds. Be simple. Planning the itinerary for a trip through Europe won't give the same effect.

Programmed Visualisation

There are two distinct schools of visualisation. In one, you 'make' the image arise. You program it. In the other, you 'let' the image arise spontaneously. Trying to project an image on a screen is a programmed visualisation.

People automatically prefer one approach over the other. One man told me he could even program his dreams. The idea of allowing images to arise freely was, however, repugnant to him.

Saint Ignatius said we should evoke selected images to make ourselves a better person. The American thought-control schools also try to program the mind. They train people to imagine themselves more confident, richer or wiser, or achieving their goals. The idea here is that thoughts have a hypnotic, almost magical, effect. Therefore, what you think or believe, good or bad, will come true.

Obviously, there is a grain of truth in this, but it is often taken to an absurd degree. I recently received a panicky phone call from a woman with cancer. 'I know I've got to stop every single negative thought,' she said. 'How can I do it?' Any meditator could tell her she was attempting the impossible.

People feel if they 'think positively', positive things will happen. Again, this Pollyanna attitude is partially true. Good thoughts are not, however, enough to stop cancer, a marriage break-up, global recession or a nuclear war. Positive thinking can be a denial of the most obvious facts. This has its dangers.

When positive thinking seems to fail, people often feel guilty. They feel, obviously, their faith wasn't strong enough. They let the negatives creep in and they are paying the price. In these cases, positive thinking and visualisation are more a kind of religious faith, or superstition, than a meditation practice. It is rarely subjected to any kind of reality check.

Spontaneous Visualisation

Programmed visualisation is a kind of forceful thinking. St Ignatius regarded it as an 'exercise of the will'. It is close to the beta brainwave state. Spontaneous visualisation, however, is more relaxed. It is closer to alpha than beta, and can activate the dream consciousness.

Most people find it easier to work with the freely arising images. We may not be able to evoke a perfect white rose and fix it like a photograph on a wall. If we put in a request, however, the mind may deliver something. It may not be a rose — possibly a daisy or camellia will come up instead. And it may be pink or yellow. Perhaps it is fully open and past its prime. There may be some bruising on the outer petals. And there is a bug inside …

Most meditations are clear and logical practices. Visualising, however, is very idiosyncratic, especially when you work with freely arising images. Images often come up spontaneously in the course of a meditation, and can be fun to work with.

It may interest you to know how I learnt to visualise. For years I was a 'cool' meditator. I watched the breath and the body rigorously, and ignored any images that arose. I was a pure sensation meditator, 'in touch with reality', with no frills.

I felt something was lacking, however, so I took up the practices of Tibetan Buddhism. My training involved literally tens of thousands of prostrations, mantras and accompanying visualisations. This was not at all what I thought of as meditation.

Even worse, I apparently couldn't visualise at all. I sympathise completely with students who say: 'I never see anything when I try to visualise.' I was trying to picture male and female deities, crystal palaces, colours, trees, animals, jewels, energy flows in the body—and I was getting nothing at all.

Yet I doggedly persisted, with little hope, and suddenly it happened. It was like a door flying open. The imagery had always been there. I just hadn't looked in the right direction. The images didn't replace or compete with 'reality'. They were like a superimposition, or a double image over-laying it. Once I knew how to look, the memory bank opened. Memories arose, with extraordinary detail, from earlier and earlier in my youth and childhood. The well of memories upon which to draw was inexhaustible.

Over the years, the images have changed. The parade of images of youth, childhood and infancy has largely finished. Instead the images now arise from some place beyond my personal history. Jung would call it the 'collective unconscious'. Buddhism calls it the 'storehouse consciousness'. It is like dream imagery, but even more strange, subtle and diverse than ordinary dreams.

And it is always there. Our minds are continually generating multi-sensual imagery. We don't notice it because our conscious mind is too busy with trivia. The stars are always in the sky, but we don't see them when the sun is out. We usually notice this imagery only in a dream or at the edge of sleep.

I had always been fascinated by dreams. Now I discovered some part of the mind is always dreaming, day and night, even as I ate breakfast, answered the telephone and worked on the computer.

Where Am I? What Is This?

A dream, and the inner imagery, is often a comment from within on what is happening in our lives. It generally tells us what is out of balance. We don't have to go to sleep to hear these messages. Here are a couple of 'first aid' practices. They are quite useful if you are feeling bad.

Just ask yourself: 'Where am I?' Sense your body and allow an image to arise that expresses the physical/emotional feeling. It is usually quite a relief just to crystallise the feeling in an image. This is what some students have said:

'There is a lead ball in my stomach.'

'I feel like a crushed tin can.'

'I feel like I'm being pulled apart by wild horses.'

Here is a similar exercise. When something is disturbing you, ask 'What is this?' and then wait for an image that illustrates it. Recently, I put the phone down after an amicable conversation, but felt awful. So I asked, 'What is this?' The image soon came. It was like I had eaten mouldy fruitcake (the unconscious has a great sense of humour). This image brought some insight as well. The woman I spoke to had great ability (the richness of the fruitcake), which was flawed by her manipulative nature (the mould). The image told me how I was instinctively responding to her.

Getting Quality in Your Visualisation

We can all fantasise and imagine things without knowing how to meditate. A good visualisation, however, should be more than daydreaming and wishful thinking.

Students tend to enjoy the images. As a teacher, however, I am more interested in their quality of mind. A good meditation should make the mind relaxed, clear, undistracted and capable of good focus. The meditation object is just a means towards this end.

Visualisers are often so entranced by the images, or trying so hard, they don't notice their quality of mind. Often it is excited, overactive, anxious and manipulative. They tend to believe the image is more important than their underlying mind state. They seek the golden eggs, but forget to feed the goose.

I often meet people who visualise in a tight, controlled way that doesn't feel meditative to me. In any meditation, we should first aim for an open, gentle, receptive state of mind. Because visualising draws on the dream consciousness, it is easier to visualise when we are already quite relaxed.

I am often asked if there are meditations for curing cancer. There are. Ninety per cent of the benefits of a meditation, however, come from being able to relax deeply with a clear mind. Fear, anger and desire all vanish when we relax well. At such times, we are at peace with ourselves and the world. What could be more healthy than to spend hours in that state?

When we relax, healing visualisations (such as the 'white light' meditation on pages 96–97) can enhance this effect. If the person cannot even relax, however, a visualisation will be little more than a 'feel-good' head trip. This is not without value, but it is unlikely to cure cancer, for example.

MEDITATION: VISUALISATION

Possible Objects

You can imagine anything you like. Generally speaking, complex visualisation or ones that progress in time, like a story, can be good for beginners. They tend to keep you engaged. The simpler images, however, will actually take you deeper. They allow the mind to become more settled and focused.

You can visualise very casually. If an image arises in a meditation, then use it as a temporary point of focus, just as you could use a sound or a pain in the body. You examine it with dispassion, noticing colour, shape and detail. Stay sensual and avoid the temptation to think about it. Don't get attached to it. Let it go as soon as it fades and return to your original meditation object.

You can visualise more formally. It is common to work with colours and natural objects at first. If you want to evoke colour, you can prime yourself by deciding to notice all the yellow or red things, for example, you see during the day. When you sit to meditate, it should be much easier then to evoke red or yellow.

To evoke colour, it is often helpful to imagine an object of that colour. You could go through the colours of the spectrum this way, imagining in turn a red tomato, an orange orange, a yellow daffodil, a green leaf, the blue of the sky, and so on.

You can evoke objects. Familiar things are best at first. Imagine an apple, a cup, a flower, a candle, a stone. It often helps to have these physically in front of you as you meditate, so you can open your eyes and look at them occasionally.

You can evoke places. Imagine your living room, the walk to work or your friend's house. Everyday places are a good point with which

MEDITATION: VISUALISATION (continued)

to start. Alternatively, go to a place that was good for you. It could be a natural scene, a place you went on holiday or some house from the past where you were particularly happy.

You can evoke people — a lover, friend or relative. It could be someone you have never met, but whom you admire. The good feeling you raise helps you stay focused.

Instructions

- Loosen up the body and the breathing. When you are ready, call up an image or colour or place. Don't force it. Just allow it to emerge in its own time.
- Be playful with the image. Gently explore the detail. Let the mood wash through you and change your body chemistry. If you wish, you could 'name' your meditation object each time you breath out. You could say 'red' or 'rose' or 'Bali' or 'Claire', rather like an affirmation to help you stay on track.
- Know that you will relax more deeply if you don't 'think' too much. Be sensual rather than thoughtful. Don't fan up the feeling or get too excited. Conserve your energy and let the mind settle into the object.
- If the image fades, hold the memory of it for a few seconds. Don't struggle, however, to make it 'come back'. Return to the breath, or enjoy the space when the image disappears. Be content with nothing. The mind can be quite peaceful when all thoughts and images fade.
- If you want, evoke another image, or notice if another image is waiting in the background.
- Occasionally, check that you are not becoming too active (this is the usual problem with visualisation). Check that your body and mind are actually relaxing. Keep some detachment towards the object. Don't get passionate about it. Regard it as just another prop for the mind to hold on to, like the breath or a mantra.

CHAPTER 16

Being Present

A Zen master was once asked, 'How often do you meditate?' He answered, 'When am I not meditating?' Obviously his understanding of meditation differed from that of the questioner. Even a master has to eat and go to the toilet, gets angry and sad occasionally, has to deal with difficult people, and sickens and dies. Is it really possible for him to 'meditate' through all of that?

If he really is a master, he can. He can embrace the pleasure and pain of life completely. He is relaxed in the sense that he is afraid of nothing and doesn't want anything he hasn't got. He has no axe to grind with the imperfections of the moment. He is always awake — and always at peace with what life brings him.

If one word describes meditation, it is *awareness*. This means being awake while awake, or to know what is happening in the moment. St Theresa was once criticised for eating perch with obvious gusto. She said, 'When I pray, I pray. When I eat fish, I eat fish.' She didn't eat fish trying to look as if she was praying. Being relaxed means being in harmony with the situation in which you find yourself. If you can't relax, the problem (and the solution) is not 'out there'. It is in you.

Formal meditation is just square one. It is just practice — not the real thing. After all, meditation is tranquil. Life isn't. We cannot, however, run from life forever. It has a habit of muscling in. Meditation should be a preparation for, not an escape from, life. The secret is to weave the stillness and detachment of meditation into the turbulence of our daily lives.

First we find we can remain relaxed and alert with our eyes open. Then we are relaxed and alert while walking in the park or on the beach, and then, in turn, while doing simple exercises such as preparing a meal or having a shower. Soon we find we can stay calm when someone presses our buttons. Boring tasks become less irksome. We appreciate moments of beauty in the midst of turmoil and have moments of clarity even in strong emotion.

Being Calm and Clear in All Circumstances

Beginners often have little flexibility at first. They say 'I couldn't meditate because ...':

- a dog was barking;
- I could hear the television next door;
- I had a stomach ache;
- I've got too much on my mind;
- I'm angry with my ex-husband;
- It was a long day. I am too tired.

Eventually they realise it is all grist for the mind. Meditation doesn't magically dispel the pain and take you into bliss. It only enables you to find the point of balance. A meditator doesn't calm the waves. He or she just floats like a cork on the ups and downs.

So, how do you stay afloat? A Zen master is awake. We, on the other hand, like to operate on automatic pilot. This gives the mind a break. It is restful, but it blurs our perception of reality and so it is a mixed blessing. We can shuffle through the day not sensing or feeling anything clearly. What is worse, we can be too dull to realise it. We may not even know what we were thinking a moment ago. Some days, we're just not here at all. No wonder we have problems, and are so confused by them.

Just because we wake up in the morning doesn't mean we are fully here. Awareness doesn't come automatically. It helps to practise it. The best place to start is to be present. This means noticing the sights, sounds, smell, tastes and tactile sensations of the moment.

Turning Simple Activities into Meditations

This is kitchen-sink meditation. I often meditate while preparing food. Sometimes I focus on one sense, such as sound. I listen to each sound I make: cutting the apple, putting the knife down, the squeal of the tap and the water running, the bowl scraping on the bench, a foot shuffle, the refrigerator door opening, the clang as I place something on a rack, and so on. I hold my mind to the task by saying the word 'sound' silently, each time I breathe out. I am aware of other sensations, of course, but I highlight the sounds.

Alternatively, I notice input from any sense: the texture of the knife, fruit, water or the door handle; the glistening skin of a capsicum, patterns of light and shadow, a stain on the bench; or the sensations in my arm as I lift something. I non-verbally ask myself: 'Where is my mind, right now?' It is amazing how rapidly my mind can disappear into thought. And how interesting the sense world can be if we focus on it.

The Japanese tea ceremony is a sensory meditation. As the guest, you watch each movement of the tea-maker. You enjoy the room, hear the sounds, watch the steam, feel and look at the bowl, taste the tea and feel yourself swallowing. You become tranquil by focusing on one minute detail after another.

The Buddha said: 'When walking, just walk. When eating, just eat. Similarly when standing, sitting, getting dressed or going to the toilet.' Our problem is that when walking, we think about work. At work, we think about sex. When with our lover or spouse, we think about last night's television. When watching television, we also eat, read the newspaper and talk to someone. It is not surprising the mind gets confused and exhausted, and we don't enjoy the television, the food or making love as much as we could.

Another Zen master said, 'Miraculous activity! — chopping wood and drawing water.' If we can't find happiness in this very moment, where will be find it? We are often tense because we always want to be somewhere else, doing something different.

Because being present seems like a good idea, you may resolve: 'Today, I am going to live in the present!' It takes a lifetime, however, to be a Zen master. It is best to be more modest in your goals.

Don't try to be present for an hour or a day. Just try for a few seconds or minutes at a time. It can be surprisingly satisfying. Try to eat a biscuit consciously. Enjoy watering your plants. Brush your teeth deliberately. Each of these can be very pleasant, simply because other thoughts remain backstage and the mind enjoys doing one thing at once.

This kind of meditation has no boundaries. It doesn't require a quiet room and half an hour carved out of the day. Anywhere and anytime will do. You could make any of the following into a meditation.

- **Hanging out the washing**
  (Feel the wet cloth, the varying weights, the pegs, the wind on your face, the body sensations of bending and stretching, catching glimpses of the sky ...)

- **Getting dressed or undressed**
  (Body movement, texture of the clothing, the sounds of skin against cloth ...)

- **Having a shower**
  (The smell of soap, sound of the water, pleasure, warmth, wet skin, the texture of the towel, dry stimulated skin ...)

- **Walking to the supermarket**
  (Parking the car, turning off the ignition, sounds of opening and closing doors, walking across the lot, noticing the sky and the trees, shaking the trolley loose ...)

Many of us choose to be more or less unaware. Instead of noticing the beauty of life, we switch on the television and read the paper. Often it takes an illness such as cancer to make people wake up. Such people often say they suddenly see what is important — feeling the dawn air, walking around the garden, a moment with a friend.

To be more aware is like switching on the light — but it has a price. It illuminates not just the beauty, but the mess and confusion of life as well. So the Zen master gets angry and watches his anger come and go. He is relaxed with his anger. He feels sadness without being dragged down by it. He feels pain without self-pity or fear. Anyone who has been near a great teacher knows how human they are. They are not serene, smiling, plaster saints at all. They could be more peaceful if they choose to numb themselves out, like the rest of humanity tend to do. They choose, however, to be fully alive instead.

MEDITATION: BEING PRESENT

Being present means focusing on the sensations of the moment—sight, sound, smell, taste or touch. Usually we focus on just one thing, such as the breath or music. Focusing on any sensation, however, will bring you into the present.

In this meditation, you focus on whatever sensation catches your attention. When some other sensation becomes more obvious, you move to that. If you want, you can multi-layer your meditation: being aware of breath, sounds and sight simultaneously. Often it is good to primarily focus on the breath, but assimilate other sensations as they arise.

Instructions

- Sit down and relax the body and breathing as usual.
- Notice what is the strongest sensation and focus on it. It could be the breath, or a pain in the shoulder, or a lawnmower outside.
- Gently explore the detail of it. Feel your breathing relaxing into it.
- Soon, you notice something else is pushing into the mind. Perhaps your head is aching a little, or your eyes fall on a pot plant opposite. Pay attention to that instead. Give it at least a few seconds.
- Don't go searching, but, when another sensation becomes obvious, shift your attention to that. Know that the longer you stay with something, the deeper you relax. If you find something you enjoy, or your basic meditation object is calling you, then stay with that. Nonetheless, don't struggle to hold one thing when something else is more vivid.
- Check yourself occasionally. Ask yourself, 'Am I in the present?' or 'Where is the mind right now?' Notice if your body is relaxing, and enjoy what you experience.

CHAPTER 17

Staying Awake While Going to Sleep

We have all seen cartoon images of the perfect meditator. He sits effortlessly in full lotus on a mountain top, oblivious to the cares of the world. His thoughts, if any, are radiant and blissful. He seems light years away from you, as you try to meditate in your untidy bedroom, tired and irritable after a day at work. *I'll never be able to meditate*, you think, as you succumb to one aggravating thought after another.

Most meditation takes place with an awareness of peripheral thoughts and sensations. Just occasionally, however, we drop beyond all that. We get a taste of something special and unique. We think, *That's what that yogi on the mountain feels like!*

These beautiful states usually happen just at the edge of sleep. This is when the metabolism slows down, the body is perfectly still and the last thoughts dissolve into the surrounding space. We call this the 'body asleep, mind awake' state. It is exquisite, but difficult to hold.

In the East, meditation is the path of 'awakening'. This means, in part, staying awake as the body goes to sleep. This goes against all our conditioning. Usually when the body starts falling asleep, the mind follows. By losing consciousness, however, we stumble at the threshold and miss the deeper states of mind.

Stages of Depth

In the East, there are considered to be four classical stages of awakening. These are to be:

- awake while awake;
- awake while dreaming;
- awake in dreamless sleep; and
- to integrate all three at once.

The first stage of awakening, being awake while awake, means to be present, or to be fully aware of thoughts, feelings and sensations the moment they arise. This takes practice. Some people seem to sleepwalk through life. We can drive across town on automatic pilot, and even work or relate to people in the same way. When our mind is consumed by unconscious anxieties or fantasy, we may be 'absentminded' most of the day.

The second stage is to be awake while dreaming. We approach this through the 'body asleep, mind awake' state. This is quite volatile. Most of us only peer over the threshold occasionally. I'll describe this in more detail shortly.

The third stage is to be awake in dreamless sleep. This is deep trance, but is still a conscious state. The metabolic rate drops very low; the brain emits the very slow, delta brainwaves; the breathing seems to stop and you lose the sense of self and body completely. You are conscious, but there are no images or thoughts in consciousness.

It is a state of unimaginable peace and delight. It is described as being one with God or the Universal Mind. Tibetans call it the 'pregnant void', or the emptiness out of which all things arise.

Mystics tend to regard this as the end of the spiritual journey. Yet it still has shortcomings. It doesn't last. You still come back to your toothache and sore back, and you still have to find your daily bread.

The fourth stage is to integrate all three states at once. It is like living in parallel realities. This is to experience the indescribable bliss of the third stage, while arguing with your three-year-old over breakfast. In the waking state, it is important to have matching socks. In the deep sleep state, you could watch the destruction of galaxies with equanimity and certainly couldn't care less about socks.

If you can integrate all three states, however, you still go out to look for the other sock.

Balancing on the Threshold

Let us go back to the 'body asleep, mind awake' state. It usually takes years before you can hold your mind steady in the dream state. It is easy, however to get glimpses of it. We cross the threshold every night, as we go into or come out of sleep.

It is that in-between state, when we couldn't honestly say we were either awake or asleep. It usually occurs as we are struggling to waken or collapsing into the darkness. Sometimes, however, perhaps after waking from a light afternoon sleep, the mind feels bright, delicate and fresh. For a moment, there are no thoughts at all. You are conscious, but may not even know where you are or what time it is.

Conversely, we may notice this state while falling asleep. We may still be just awake, but dream images or irrational thoughts flit by. These *hypnagogic* images are usually very brief, come in clusters and are often weirder than our usual dreams. We are dreaming while still awake.

The way we perceive our bodies also changes in this state. While awake, we are always aware of our body and its location in space. We look after it. When asleep, however, we completely abandon it. In fact, we actually abandon it in stages. A meditator can watch the process of the body falling asleep.

For example, when we first lie on the bed, we are usually still engaged in thought — a beta-brainwave state. The body feels solid, the way it usually does. As thoughts subside, we shift into alpha and sensing mode. We are aware of the room and the sheets against our skin. The body now feels softer. As we relax a little more, however, the boundaries of our body dissolve. We lose contact with arms and legs. We may know we are still awake, but not know if we are lying on our left or right sides. We don't know if we are touching our partner or not. Our body is disappearing, part by part.

Yet we are still conscious. We are not inert and dead. We still feel the subtle vibrations of being alive — spacious, tingling and warm, like the hum of the cells — which seem to be everywhere and nowhere. It has a mood also, even if we don't put it into words. It is something like 'God! This is lovely.' Then you fall fast asleep and lose it.

People particularly notice this 'body asleep, mind awake' state in guided meditations. They say things such as: 'I seemed to be asleep, but I know I was awake. I could hear every word you said.' Sometimes they say: 'I could hear you talking, but you seemed very far away.'

They were dropping into sleep. Every time I spoke, however, it woke them up a little and kept their heads above water. They would relax, then pull back, relax and pull back, until they were balancing on the threshold between waking and sleep. Occasionally, someone will say, 'I must have fallen asleep about fifty times.'

In that state, their bodies are asleep. A technician monitoring their metabolism and brain activity would say that person was asleep. Yet they were obviously still awake. They didn't fall off their chairs.

It is easy to taste this state, but difficult to stabilise it. Usually the mind lurches between thoughts, dream images and unconsciousness at first. People often have an inner battle. They want to follow their lifelong conditioning and collapse into sleep. At the same time, they want to enjoy this state, which means staying awake.

Eventually, you realise it is best to stay awake. It is not an either/or choice. If you stay awake, you get the best of both worlds. You get deeper relaxation and more mental clarity. When you can hold that state, it is delightful. It is serene, clear and timeless. You have entered the palace of the gods.

The beauty of this state is that thoughts have almost completely disappeared. People often ask me in frustration and despair, 'How can I block out my thoughts? They are driving me crazy!' There are only three good ways I know. All require practice, unfortunately.

The first is to become intently absorbed in something sensual. The second is to disengage from thoughts the moment they arise, by naming or 'just watching' them. The third is to be mentally alert as the body goes to sleep.

The Transpersonal States

When awake, we are inescapably conscious of self. 'Do I need to patch up my make-up? ... I don't like what she said to me.... Shall I have another beer? ...' We evaluate every incoming sensation as either good for us, bad for us or irrelevant. The universe revolves around us.

When we relax deeply, however, we step outside this mental soap opera. The 'body asleep, mind awake' state takes us beyond self. We remain conscious, but we lose consciousness of self. We enter the 'transpersonal' states.

Achaan Chaa, the great Thai teacher, said:

If you let go a little, you have a little peace.
If you let go a lot, you have a lot of peace
If you let go completely, you have complete peace.

You let go most completely in the 'body asleep, mind awake' state. If the mind also went to sleep, your thoughts would enslave you. If you stay awake, however, your thoughts and anxieties can't get a foothold. They evaporate the moment they surface, without going underground. The feeling is literally 'ecstatic', in the sense of 'standing outside' yourself. In this state, you stand outside the 'I, me, mine', self-orientated thoughts. It is pure delight.

In the transpersonal state, the body has virtually vanished. You know it is there somewhere, but can't feel it. With no sense of body or self, there is no fear and no anger. There is nothing there to be hurt. There is also no desire or longing. What else could you possibly want? You have it all.

Because no thoughts — not even unconscious ones — are agitating the mind, your metabolism can slow down very quickly. Within minutes, a meditator can drop his metabolic rate to the lowest point possible. It might take hours to reach this stage with normal sleep. This is why meditation, minute for minute, relaxes the body more deeply than sleep.

Simply to be relaxed is good for your health. Meditation is good medicine, but some ailments need high dosages. Dramatic cures of life-threatening illness are more likely if you can enter the transpersonal states. In these states, there is just pure awareness, love and acceptance. This cuts off the chronic emotional negativities that make us sicker than we need to be.

As the body relaxes, it releases bound-up energy. People actually use meditation like a health food bar, to give them a boost during the day. We usually spend this extra energy on thought or fantasy or action.

You can, however, use this energy for enhanced clarity of mind. Only a mind of crystal clarity and split-second awareness can take you into the trance states. I find it difficult to persuade people this is worth doing. Most of us could do with more rest than we get, so our tendency is to fall asleep or fantasise when we get this relaxed.

If you keep the lights on while descending into sleep, you see how vast and astonishing the mind is. It is bigger, stronger and wiser than the Internet. The conscious mind seems small and fussy in comparison. Once you peek into the transpersonal states, you realise meditation is much more than a New Age sedative to help you relax and sleep better.

MEDITATION: BODY ASLEEP, MIND AWAKE

This is the most effective meditation I know for taking people into the 'body asleep, mind awake' state. People with insomnia often use it deliberately to go to sleep.

Its other name is *yoga nidra*, which means 'yoga sleep'. It is designed to induce a light, conscious trance state as close to sleep as possible. People often do it at the end of a yoga class. They lie down comfortably, the teacher talks them through and within seconds most of the class is dead to the world. They have a good sleep, but a poor meditation.

This is a body-scanning practice with a difference. You shift your point of focus every few seconds, or with each breath or two. It works on the principle that the mind is always alert when it notices something new. If you hear a new sound, or someone new walks by, the mind wakes up and pays attention. Once the stimuli is assessed, the mind goes back to its thinking or daydreaming or whatever it was doing before.

So, you focus on your thumb, for example. Before you have time to get bored with it, you shift to the next finger. The sensations are slightly different, so they hold your attention for a second at least. Then you let go again and move to the next finger, and so on. The mind stays alert, noticing new things. And the quick changes make it hard to think systematically about anything else.

Because this meditation involves a lot of focusing, you stay alert. Because you can't think much about other things, you relax deeply.

MEDITATION: BODY ASLEEP, MIND AWAKE (continued)

This gives you the best of both worlds. The mind is alert, but the body goes to sleep.

The meditation may seem complicated, but it is easy to learn. It is sequential. (As the old song says 'the hip bone is connected to the thigh bone ...') It may help to record it on tape yourself., or you could order a tape from the Perth Meditation Centre.

It consists of four parts. First you move through the right side of the body. You move through the fingers, up the arm, down the right side of the back and the legs to the right little toe. Then you pause for about a minute.

You then repeat this with the left side. And pause for a minute. Then move up the back of the body from the feet to the crown of the head and down to the face. And pause. Finally, you move down through the internal organs, and settle on the breath.

Instructions

- If you want to stay awake, sit up in a chair. If you want to go to sleep, then lie down. Spend a few seconds relaxing the body and the breathing.
- Starting moving your mind like a spotlight around the body. Shift location with each breath or two. Name each place and try to feel or imagine the sensations there, however subtle. The parts may tingle slightly as you focus on them. Move lightly, sensing and letting go, sensing and letting go. Sensing is enough. You don't have to make each part relax.

RIGHT SIDE: 'Right thumb ... forefinger ... middle finger ... ring finger ... little finger ... back of the hand ... palm ... wrist ... forearm ... elbow ... upper arm ... shoulder ... right upper back ... middle back ... lower back ... buttock ... thigh ... knee ... lower leg ... ankle and heel ... sole ... top of the foot ... big toe ... second toe ... third toe ... fourth toe ... little toe ...'

MEDITATION: BODY ASLEEP, MIND AWAKE (continued)

Pause for about a minute, sensing the whole right side of the body. Notice if it feels different from the left.

LEFT SIDE: 'Left thumb ... to left little toe' as above, and pause for about a minute.

BACK OF THE BODY: 'Both feet and ankles (trying to feel them from inside) ... both lower legs and knees ... thighs and hips ... belly and lower back ... chest and upper back ... hands and arms ... shoulders, neck and throat ... back and sides of the head ... crown of the head and forehead ... the eyes and behind the eyes ... the ears and inside the ears ... nose and cheeks ... mouth and jaw ...'

Pause for about a minute, sensing the whole face and the whole body.

INSIDE THE BODY: 'Inside the nasal passages ... inside the mouth, feeling tongue, teeth and saliva ... inside the throat ... inside the right lung (feeling it expand and contract) ... inside the left lung (does that feel any different from the right?) ... heart ... liver ... stomach ... kidneys ... intestines ... sexual organs ... the whole inside of the body.'

- Let your mind rest wherever it wants to in the body. Feel the flow of the breath or the pulsing of the heart for the remainder of the meditation.

CHAPTER 18

Emotional Healing

We occasionally hear of 'miracle' cures through meditation. These are rare, but do happen. In the East, terminally ill people often say goodbye to their family and go to a monastery to die. A few, however, are still alive years later, hale and hearty. Their emotional entanglements and social identity had made them sick. By cutting free, they became healthy again.

Such people rarely return to their former lives. They healed because there was 'a deep turning in the seat of consciousness'. Their psyche was reorientated from emotional disease to emotional health. Their meditation was not a kind of psychic surgery that cut out the illness, leaving their personality intact. Slowly, gradually and thoroughly, it changed them completely.

The Emotional Causes of Ill Health

The causes of stress and consequent ill health seem to be manifold. A tough life and 'lifestyle' factors, poor living or working conditions, genes, difficulties in relationships, major disappointments, our conditioning, our unnatural modern lives all seem to blame. There is, however, a more fundamental cause. It is in the way we react.

Some people are able to find great serenity and joy in concentration camps or during war. Others are paralysed with anxiety in the midst of trouble-free lives. Whether we live in heaven or hell largely depends on our response to life.

Life is often painful. We all carry wounds — big, small and invisible ones. If we fully accept what has happened and is happening, we can be psychologically healthy. If we react negatively to what life offers, we squirm like a worm on a hook, trapped by chronic fear, anger or desire. These choked emotions permeate the mind and are rarely released or fully satisfied. They slowly, but inexorably, poison us over years. They corrode the soul and damage the body. Emotional blockage is the main psychological cause of sickness.

Meditation leads you to emotional health in two ways. First, by 'just watching', you notice the old emotion within you and allow it to surface. This has a purgative effect. By opening your heart to pain, you allow it to release. Secondly, by relaxing deeply and consciously, you go beyond your preoccupation with self and enter transpersonal states that, in an emotional sense, are extraordinarily healthy. By 'just watching' you liberate old emotion. By relaxing deeply, you nourish yourself with healthy new emotion.

How the Body Is Purified of Old Emotion

We often don't know the difference between healthy and unhealthy emotions. We assume, for example, that anger is unhealthy and love is good for us. This misses the point completely. Every emotion, however unwelcome, is healthy in its basic impulse. It becomes poisonous only when it is blocked or ignored. The source of most stress is blocked or frozen emotion.

Blocking emotion is a good short-term strategy. We should all be able to postpone our emotional release if we need to—but we can only *postpone* it. The emotion doesn't vanish. It goes underground and waits. It is always trying to surface, even if it is decades old. It has good company in our underground pool of old pain and sorrow. If it can't come through as emotion, it can build to a critical mass and emerge as sickness in the body.

When the mind becomes peaceful and spacious in a meditation, old emotion may arise. The trauma of a marriage separation or the loss of a parent in childhood may surface. You first feel a vague discontent rising within you. This is uncomfortable, but, if you can 'just watch' it, it eventually bursts into the light of day.

It is like a boil surfacing, and then bursting, on the skin. If you don't block the pain as you did in the past, it releases. This can happen very quickly. The more intense it is, the quicker it is over. Pain that is decades old will sometimes vanish in seconds or minutes.

All you have to do is watch with detachment. It is like weeping and yelling internally, while also watching yourself weep or yell. You let the emotion express itself as it wishes. You don't need to amplify it or make sense of it. Once you understand the process, it is quite awesome. The mind knows exactly what is necessary for healing. Whenever the mind is strong and spacious, it will throw out more of the inner toxins.

The process is cyclic. On retreat, people often have two or three days of deepening calm and clarity. Then, for a few hours or a day, their shadow stuff emerges. It is often awkward to handle, but it passes. People then have another two or three days of increasing calm, and the process repeats.

This is the process of *purification*, to put a pretty name on a messy event. When it is crude, it is more like psychological vomiting or diarrhoea. You feel the inner choking of emotion, the build-up and gagging, and finally the release. You feel good, but a little weak and overcome. Despite this description, it is a subtle phenomenon. You may see no sign of it happening if you look casually at a meditator from the outside.

Emotions Want To Move Out

Emotions are very physical things. Each is a precise cocktail of hormones that triggers effects in the body. It can be useful to see emotions as wanting to move either up or down in the body. Anger is a hard, upward movement. Joy is a soft, upward expansion. Fear is a hard, downward contraction. Sorrow is a soft, downward expansion.

The word *emotion* literally means 'to move out'. An impulse arises in the core of our being and wants to move outwards. If we don't block this movement, it moves through and physical equilibrium returns. We see this tension and release occur very quickly in little children.

The process, however, is like a fever. It can incapacitate us for a few seconds or minutes, if we surrender to it completely. This creates difficulties. A person giving way to grief, anger or desire is temporarily uncivilised. They are unable to work or get the kids off to school.

Most full expressions of emotion will not be tolerated by the people around you. (Rightly so, I might add. Most strong emotion is blind.) It may satisfy your body to vent your rage, but the downstream consequences may be catastrophic. So, we freeze our emotion, or leak it out in small doses over days. Unfortunately, the deep freeze eventually overloads and breaks down — often when we are in our thirties or forties.

I once analysed a dream in which exactly this image arose. A woman dreamt that her refrigerator had broken down. When she looked in the freezer, she found the dismembered corpse of her estranged husband. It was starting to thaw. She realised this spoke of the way she 'froze up' years earlier. She left her husband because she couldn't cope with his sickness. She also felt this was the source of her recurring skin cancers. It was now seven years later, and she was stronger. To be healthy, she had to let the corpse of those frozen feelings thaw.

How To Recognise Healthy or Unhealthy Thoughts

We are so conditioned to suppress certain feelings that we often don't know what a healthy response is. It is not enough to go out and beat pillows, 'speak your truth' or try to follow moral guidelines. Meditators tune into a more direct way of knowing whether a thought or emotion is healthy or unhealthy. They read their body response. In general, a thought is healthy if it feels good in the body.

An unhealthy thought or emotional response makes the body and mind contract. They both feel tight, hard and inflexible. The emotion can't 'move out' as it needs to. The mind is usually stuck or obsessed. The whole world contracts down to a pinhead. It seems that nothing is more important than that sexy body or that grievous insult. The body and mind squirm on the hook.

A healthy thought, however, does the opposite. The body becomes soft and loose, with a sense of inner flow and movement. The mind is usually not obsessed. It is receptive to new things. If you are sensitive to your body, you should be able to read if you are tightening or loosening. The more movement or flow, the happier you will be.

So 'stuckness' is bad and movement is good. Movement is often painful, but healthy. It hurts to lance a boil, but the boil goes. Relaxing into deep sorrow is not pleasant, but the sorrow moves through. For all its intensity, strong emotion is at least subtly painful. Its natural cycle is to peak and fade away. If it peaks fully, it fades fully. If its expression is partial, however, the rest goes underground, bruised and resentful, and waiting for a chance to sneak back on stage.

By meditating, we observe the emotional flavour of our minds. It is like testing water. It may look pure, but closer examination may show it to be riddled with unhealthy emotion. If you are caught in a train of thought, ask yourself: 'What is the emotion behind this?' It is quite likely to be low-grade chronic fear, anger or desire.

Many people who try to be good are consumed by the emotions they are trying to avoid. Just as people in Third World countries can survive with contaminated water, so we can get by with contaminated minds. Our quality of life and our health, however, may be terrible.

If you are unsure whether a certain thought or emotion is healthy or not, ask yourself this question: 'If this feeling was ten times stronger, would it feel healthy or unhealthy for my body?' You may find that emotions you relish—strong desire, for example, or self-righteous indignation—are very painful in the body.

'Just Watching' the Emotions Release

Both body and mind know how to heal themselves. The process never stops. The deep part of the mind knows exactly what to do, where and when, for inner health. All we can consciously do is speed up or slow down the process.

The best strategy goes right back to our basic meditation instruction: focus on one thing and 'just watch' everything else pass by. If you 'just watch' the play of consciousness, you see yourself being transformed from within.

Being able to 'just watch', however, is a skill that takes years to perfect. Usually we either like or dislike what we see. That triggers off a subtle desire or aversion that makes the mind and body tight. Even the best of meditators try to manipulate the mind so it gives them pleasure.

It often takes meditators years to realise that 'just watching' gives better results than trying to hang on to the goodies. As you stop indulging the thousands of tiny attractions and aversions in a meditation, the pay-off is much greater. The process of transformation speeds up enormously. You shed the pain and deep happiness arises.

The inner toxins clear in stages. As you relax, you acknowledge and let go of the irritations of the day. If you meditate longer, the unprocessed detritus of the year emerges. In time, your whole life parades before you. The Buddha said that the unfinished business of your whole life passes through consciousness each seven days.

If we 'just watch' a blocked emotion, it will surface and release. If our minds are utterly clear, it can vanish in one vivid instant, like a bubble bursting. More commonly, we see it with some residual desire or aversion. In this case the release is more partial.

Emotion Can Escape in Three Ways

The toxic material emerges in at least one of three ways: as body sensation, as pure feeling or as imagery. In the body, uncomfortable sensations may come and go for no apparent reason. They can pass as waves of discomfort, tingling, itchiness, nausea, muscular vibrations, trembling, shooting pains, flushes, feeling bloated or lopsided, agitation, and so on.

Usually these sensations are gross and unpleasant in the beginning. Eventually, they become very fine and delicate. Technically, they are all called 'bliss', because they indicate the body is freeing up. In time, it really does feel blissful. The pain dissolves and the body feels alive and gently shimmering.

Although the unpleasant sensations are usually quite subtle, they can be difficult to sit through. They are often buried emotions rising on the physical plane. People who meditate primarily to feel peaceful often think something is wrong and stop. This is a mistake. Their meditation is actually bearing fruit.

One student told me of painful tightness in her upper arms when she relaxed. I suggested it might be a physical memory emerging. A few days later she got the pictures. When she was a child, her mother didn't believe in slapping her. Instead, she would grab her by the upper arms and shake her violently to rebuke her. From the day my student realised this, the pains went.

Sensations triggered by emotions feel distinctly different from a purely 'physical' sensation. It is more like an intense memory reverberating in the body. Unlike a backache caused by bad posture, for example, it can come and go in a flash. Nonetheless, it can be quite a challenge to 'just watch' it.

Garbage commonly comes through as pure feeling. When meditating, you suddenly feel contaminated and worthless. A good meditator neither thinks about, nor tries to ignore, this feeling. He or she lets it surface fully and 'just watches' it. They may even name it: 'I feel like crap just now.' This could easily be a memory of childhood humiliation.

It helps enormously if memories or images also arise. One woman said she kept getting images of some blood on bathroom tiles. I suggested it may be flagging some blocked emotion. When she got the entire picture, it was hardly surprising. When she was nine, she found her mother dead in the bath — she had killed herself by slitting her wrists. As a child, my student had coped well, but it was only as a mature adult that she could finally release the full horror of that incident.

These are clear examples of old emotion releasing through images, body sensations and feeling. We usually don't know, however, from where the feeling comes and it doesn't matter. Western psychotherapy argues that you need to be conscious of your conditioning in order to be free of it. Buddhist meditation covers the same ground, but says there is far too much of it ever to understand. There are millions of moments that shape us.

Instead, all we need to do is open fully, without aversion or attachment, to the feeling or image and let it find its own way out of the mind. There is a saying: 'Do nothing. Just watch. Let the sin liberate itself.' And it does.

At a certain point, we clear our personal history. We may have had a brutal parent or been sexually abused as a child. Then you realise, when the memory arises, it no longer triggers off the habitual resentment or shame. This is a sign that the old emotion has evaporated, leaving not a trace or afterthought behind.

The process, however, doesn't stop here. The template for our emotional predilections was laid as we grew in our mother's womb. The meditator feels the blockages here as extremely fine moods, or flavours in consciousness. Eventually the meditator can 'just watch' these also, and so break free of them.

By now, you are more psychologically healthy than you have ever been since conception. You have undercut all the possible psychological causes of a physical sickness. You still carry the scars of past trauma, but you no longer fan the fires. This is when 'miracle' cures can occur.

When in Trance, the Emotions Are Extremely Healthy

Although 'just watching' the process is the key, it is still based on that other meditation principle: focusing. The deeper the focus, the more bliss and happiness you experience. This is extremely nourishing and gives you the strength you need for the healing process.

When meditating, we usually focus on one thing and have a background awareness of the rest. Sometimes, however, we enter states of absorption and the rest vanishes. We get little tastes of it outside meditation. We may be so absorbed in the beauty of nature, or music, or occasionally in sport or dance or lovemaking, that time stands still and everything shines with an inner light. Absorption, or trance, is like the best part of this kind of experience.

Absorption is a transpersonal state. In meditation, it usually occurs when the body is asleep and the mind is awake. In such moments, the background disappears. The object alone — the breath or mantra, or whatever — fills the consciousness. All sense of self vanishes. What remains of 'you' is simply pure awareness. In those moments, you don't know your name, sex or the century in which you live.

Yet absorption is a state of clarity and bliss — it is not a white-out. As it often lasts only a few seconds, you are unlikely to get lost there. In this state, unhealthy emotion vanishes utterly, like snowflakes in a fire. There is no self to be hurt, so fear and anger disappear. It is utterly beautiful, so all desire and craving evaporate. Not the slightest aversion or attraction, conscious or unconscious, can get a foothold. This is a state of effortless love and acceptance.

Paradoxically, absorption only happens when 'you' stop trying to achieve it. If you want something, both 'you' and the 'wanting' are present in the mind, so absorption can't arise. 'Don't try to awaken,' they say in

Zen. 'Just sit.' You drop into absorption when the last of the subtle attractions and aversions vanish.

Absorption happens when 'you' disappear into the object. If you remain there, a strange thing happens. The object vanishes, also. There is simply infinite space. Originally, you were one with the object. Now you are one with nothing. You are like a cat at a mousehole, intensely alert — but even the cat has gone. This is the first stage of trance. You have merged with the background vibration of pure consciousness itself.

Actually it is always there, though we rarely notice it. It is like the background hum of the Big Bang resonating through the universe. The mind with which we do the dishes is the same as that which sees God.

In this state, the mind becomes unified. This is no small matter. The psychic energy, usually scattered, now streams in one direction, like iron shavings on a magnet. It streams up and down the spinal column. The longer we can stay in this state, the more deeply it transforms us. It affects body, mind and emotions equally.

Absorption may be felt physically as a streaming, almost liquid, light. It is described as the nectar of the gods, or 'like sugar cane juice', melting the bound energies in the spinal column. Others feel it as a blissful heat. It is described as the inner sacrificial fire that consumes all obstacles to awakening.

When the mind unifies, you become one with everything imaginable. Nothing is excluded. You feel one with God, nature and with all humanity (even those you hate). You are no longer at war with yourself or anyone or anything. Even your suffering is perfect in its own way. Nothing is lacking. What else could you possibly want?

Though usually brief, absorption or trance is an extremely healthy, life-affirming state of mind. This is when cancers may start to dissolve, or the buried grief and anger of decades may disintegrate. This state rarely lasts more than a few seconds or minutes, but its effect can be enormous. It gives you a taste of paradise — a mind utterly free of psychological negativity.

Everyday Emotional Health

In absorption, you fall in love with the object and forget everything else. In ordinary consciousness, however, you develop another kind of love. By 'just watching', you learn to tolerate and accept everything that comes into the mind. Eventually you can respect the right of every thought, feeling, sensation, human being, plant, animal and situation to exist, just as they are. You work towards a love that has no limits.

We occasionally meet people like this. Walt Whitman's biographer said it took years before he realised that Whitman never felt animosity towards anyone. Whitman was not pretending to be nice — he actually loved and appreciated every single human being he met.

Mothers can also display this love. I have seen two-year-olds whose behaviour makes them quite loathsome and unlovable, but mothers can often see beyond that. They see the human being struggling to emerge, and can give their little monsters the support they need to grow.

Of course, we would prefer to landscape our mental jungle and turn it into a well-cultivated Italian Renaissance garden. If only we could trash all those horrible thoughts and feelings, and start afresh. Yet meditators develop love by learning to accept themselves, just as they are, in this moment. This means giving space to the most miserable thoughts and sensations. They are part of us, and other people, and life itself. This may seem a hard task, but it works. It is infinitely more healthy than continuous inner conflict which, of course, usually fails.

What To Do If You Are Seriously Ill

Deep healing requires a fundamental shift in consciousness. To be given a death sentence by a doctor can start this process off. People often stop work or go to a beach cottage for weeks to take stock of themselves. This is meditation in the Western sense of 'thinking deeply about something'.

Meditation will help. A little meditation will help a little. A lot of meditation will help a lot. I would recommend at least two or three hours a day of meditation or some well-focused activity.

The quality will be crucial. To relax and let the mind wander is of limited value. To enter absorption states, or develop the clarity to 'just watch' painful thoughts and emotions arising, is much better. Good training and the support of a group or teacher is best. It is harder and slower for people to achieve good results on their own.

It may be necessary to make changes in lifestyle. If your work envelops you in negativity, get out of it. Health often requires sacrifices. Change your diet. Exercise more. Give yourself time to think and be, even if it means leaving your usual lifestyle behind.

Give yourself the support you need to let emotions arise. Support groups are good. A hard-nosed counsellor or psychotherapist, who won't just coddle you, would be even better. Meditation can give you the detachment to see clearly, but don't depend on meditation alone. Other techniques for emotional release are often useful to move the choked-up material along.

Enjoy life fully. Don't postpone your pleasures till later. For healing, you need to feel as good as possible. Pamper and indulge yourself. Pleasure is good medicine. It counteracts the physiological effects of stress. Don't get bogged down in the negatives. They may seem huge, but they still are only a part of life. You face them much better from a basis of enjoying life.

The bottom line is: do what feels healthy for the body and mind. Avoid what feels unhealthy. And know the difference between them. That is all. Nothing else matters.

MEDITATION: LOVING KINDNESS

When we are happy, we feel relaxed and friendly towards people around us. This perfectly ordinary state of mind is called 'loving kindness' by the Buddhists. It is not as intense as love, but it is a little more than just being kind.

In this meditation, you aim to cultivate this feeling of warmth, friendliness and acceptance towards yourself and all beings. It is always there, just below the surface, and very healthy for us. Often, we don't get much chance to express it, which is a pity.

Whenever we feel affectionate towards someone, our body chemistry changes. To be loving is the perfect antidote to stress and anxiety. The body feels soft and warm, and the inner juices flow. It is the complete opposite to the fear and hostility that many of us carry as a basic mind-set.

The meditation traditionally proceeds in stages. First you send love to yourself, then people you are fond of, then acquaintances, enemies and the whole world in turn. You develop a broad-spectrum, non-specific friendliness towards everything. It is like the Christian tradition of remembering everyone in your night-time prayers.

People often try too hard with this meditation. Affection can't be turned on. It has to be an overflow of your own good feeling. So build it up as much as you want, before you spread it to others. You could spend the whole meditation imagining your favourite grandchild if you wanted.

Version One

Feel your heart is warm and open, and feel loving towards yourself. You can say, or think, 'May I be well and happy' or 'May I be happy in body and mind.'

If you want, direct your good wishes to each part of the body in turn. Regard your liver, your bones, your intestines and so on with love, appreciating what they do for you.

When you feel good about yourself, give other people the overflow. Bring to mind someone you love. See him or her in your mind's eye,

MEDITATION: LOVING KINDNESS (continued)

or hold them in your heart, and say, 'May you be well and happy.' Let your natural good feeling towards them emerge.

If the feeling is strong, then be creative. Extend your loving kindness and empathy out to all: casual acquaintances, antagonists, the ants in the kitchen, the whole city, crocodiles and polar bears, the earth itself. Wish them all well.

Play with it and enjoy the good feelings. Notice how pleasant it is to be in a loving mood. If the feeling fades, don't push it. You don't have to be all-inclusive or too busy. Just go back to someone you love.

Version Two

- Relax the body while saying the mantra 'Om mani peme hung'. (It has a similar meaning to 'May you be well and happy.') Feel your heart opening, like a flower, radiating soft pink light in all directions.
- Send the sound vibration of the mantra, and the warmth of the visualisation, to every part of your body. Feel your body glowing with warmth and love.
- Bring to mind people you know while saying the mantra. 'See' them in a characteristic position or activity. Hold them in your heart, or imagine the pink light around them, or imagine a ray of light from your heart to theirs.
- When you feel you have contacted them, then let go and move on. Expand the range of your loving kindness as in the version above.

CHAPTER 19

Getting It All Together

Even without a teacher's guidance, meditation is easy in a group. You have the right space, adequate time and the support of others. Meditating on your own, however, is quite a different matter.

Meditation is quiet and subtle. The metabolic rate slows down, and very little happens in the body and mind. Because it is not a high-energy state, anything noisier in our minds or lives can blow it apart. It needs protection and support, particularly in the early days. In this chapter, I give suggestions to help you make meditation part of your life.

Making Time

Because meditation is based on very simple principles, people assume they can turn it on at will. Just knowing how to do it, however, doesn't mean you can do it when you want. Meditation is a skill. Like any skill, it gets rusty if you don't practise and improves if you do.

I suggest that beginners practise at least fifteen minutes a day, five days a week. It takes about two months to engrave the skill in memory. Over that period, you go through the ups and downs, you know yourself better, and you know what works for you.

Fifteen to twenty minutes is a natural period of time for a formal meditation. You tend to go through three stages. In the first, the mind is still chattering. In the second, you relax quickly, but get sleepy. In the third, you wake up a little and get the balance right. You are both relaxed and alert. This cycle often takes fifteen minutes or so. Of course, longer meditations are also good.

Some people naturally prefer spot meditations. They should still do fifteen minutes a day, but they can spread it out over four or five sessions:

two minutes sitting in the car in the office car park, five minutes deliberately unwinding during the lunch-break, a minute in the supermarket queue and a minute at the next red light. These short sessions have downstream effects for an hour or two later. They reset the thermostat (the rate at which you metabolise energy) at an appropriate level.

A Place To Meditate

It is good, though not essential, to have a regular time and place to meditate. Some places, like temples or churches, set up a strong supporting atmosphere, which can even be addictive (i.e. you can't seem to meditate anywhere else). On the other hand, a temporary and almost insignificant place can work just as well. When I put my cushion on the carpet, my living room instantly changes into a place to meditate.

People often use little rituals to create a sacred space. These act like post-hypnotic suggestions. They unconsciously remind you of the good meditations of the past. Sometimes they are almost invisible, like setting up the cushion or chair, sighing two or three times, putting your hands in a certain position. Even saying the first mantra or noting the first breath can trigger the mood much more rapidly than you would expect.

Other people are more elaborate. They tidy the room a little first. They may have a shower or put on clean clothes. They put soft music in the background. They light a candle or some incense. They may put something attractive in their field of vision, or sit before a little shrine.

If you have the choice, and your surroundings are pleasant, it is best to meditate outside. Being in nature takes you away from the artificiality of the modern life. On a beach, or under a tree, your mind becomes more primeval and natural.

When Is the Best Time To Meditate?

When people ask me the above question, I answer, 'Anytime'. Is there any time of day when you wouldn't benefit from being relaxed and aware? Usually people get into a groove, and meditate at similar times each day. Some are larks, some are owls. They choose times that suits their lifestyle and personalities.

Very early morning is a lovely time. Monks and nuns throughout the world enjoy rising in the small hours and meditating in the darkness before sunrise. The body and mind are refreshed, having slept, but the metabolic rate remains low. This gives a calm, clear, awake mind. Although most of us can't rise this early, morning is still a good time — but do wake up first. If you try to meditate lying in bed, you will just go back to sleep. If you have time, have a shower or a brisk walk, then meditate before the kids wake and the rest of the suburb comes to life.

We often burn energy rather quickly in the morning. We can meditate to stop it racing unnecessarily. I often meditate just before I leave the house. First, I get ready to go. Then, before I walk out the door, I meditate for a couple of minutes to collect myself. Similarly, if I arrive early where I am going, I will sit in the car and meditate for two minutes before moving on.

Many of my students who are business people will cut out ten or fifteen minutes in the middle of the day to meditate. Some are quite forthright about it. They lock the office door and lie on the floor or a couch. Others are more discreet, choosing to meditate in a park at lunchtime rather than eating at a noisy cafeteria.

I generally discourage people from meditating while driving, although I do know people who do it. Beginners often assume meditation is a sleepy, blanked-out state, regardless of what I say. Obviously, this can be dangerous while driving. If you are alert, however — in the present, paying attention to what you are doing and enjoying the scenery — driving can be a safe and pleasant way of relaxing. If you meditate while driving, then make 'driving' your meditation object.

People often tell me it is hard to meditate at home. Many people find it best actually to meditate in the car. They pull over at a park or a beach on their way home and just sit there, letting themselves unwind. One woman told me she goes out to the garage and sits in the car to meditate. 'The quietest place in the house,' she said.

It is excellent to meditate after arriving home from work. This is often a messy meditation, as the garbage of the day parades through. This kind of meditation helps you leave work at work, and helps you reclaim your evening. A meditation at 6 p.m. often gives you an energy charge. You find you can do useful things in the evening rather than just watching television.

Meditating before sleep can be scrappy, but useful. By noticing and detaching from the problems of the day, you don't take a sackful of problems to bed with you. It is important, however, not to meditate too long. If you do, it will refresh you and, when you go to bed, you find yourself wide awake. Five to ten minutes is usually safe. Let that downward momentum carry you into sleep.

You can meditate to put yourself to sleep. I do. If you wake in the night, you can meditate to fall asleep again. The secret is to meditate well. Don't try to waffle your way into sleep. It can help to lie on your back.

If you have woken in the night, you have probably rested enough to go on thinking for hours. To get clear of the thoughts, you need good focus. People generally say a mantra, or listen to music, or do the 'Body asleep, mind awake' meditation. If you are sitting up, a meditation keeps you alert. Exactly the same meditation will put you to sleep if you are lying down.

'I haven't time to meditate!' people often complain. I don't believe them. We usually fill our days with compulsive activity. One student said her life was too busy with full-time work and managing a family as well. I almost believed her. She did seem frantic. Halfway through the course, she gave up her job and suddenly had an extra forty hours a week. Yet she still complained, 'I can't find the time.'

We don't have to carve a twenty-minute hunk out of each day. The day is full of gaps. The trick is to notice them and use them. Ask yourself, many times a day, 'When can I meditate?' Eventually you will find the spaces. If meditation becomes a habit, like brushing your teeth, it will no longer seem like something extra that you 'have to do'. It only takes a few minutes. The benefits are that you function better, you require less sleep and sleep better, you are more content and healthier and enjoy life more. Those few minutes soon pay for themselves.

Evaluating Your Practice

I often hear comments like 'That didn't work' or 'It wasn't as good as yesterday.' Unrealistic expectations and self-criticism can be your worst enemies when trying to meditate. Don't assume that a meditation should always make you happy, peaceful and free of worries. That is asking far too much.

Here are some guidelines for evaluating your practice. Just look for improvement, not perfection. You may feel miserable at the end, but you may have been in hell at the beginning. So that was a good meditation. Ask yourself:

- Am I in a better state now than when I started?
- Am I more in the present and in touch with myself?
- Have I physically relaxed?
- Is the mind less busy, and more settled?

Don't expect too much. Plodding, workmanlike sessions often bear fine fruit two or three days later. Conversely, you can coast for a few days without practising. You may feel fine, but are using the credit you have built up. A crash usually follows, and takes another two or three days to repair.

Don't expect every meditation to be perfect. Meditating is like learning to ride a bike. You have to fall off scores of times before you can confidently sail down the road. You have to chalk up those 'failures' to get to the 'successes'.

Attend Groups and Talk to Meditators

A regular group will give you quality time and space: no distractions, no kids, no phone, a supportive place and supportive people. A weekly meditation group can give you the lift you need to practise at home regularly. Being around other meditators is inspiring. You can see what meditation is about, in the flesh. Without good people contact, your practice can be insipid.

Everything I know about meditation, I learnt from people — teachers, students and friends. Even now, my students teach me as much as I teach them. The right people provide the best learning space you can find.

Meditators can tend to be too solitary and narrow-minded. They find a practice or group that more or less works for them, and they never look beyond it. Religious groups, of course, foster this dependency to hold their followers.

Moreover, there is a tradition that you should never discuss your meditation with anyone except the teacher. I find this attitude a terrible hindrance to growth. It fosters isolation, misunderstanding and self-doubt, and incidentally gives great power to the teacher.

For these reasons, I actively encourage discussion in my classes. If we share experiences, and listen to others, we learn. Meditation should increase our critical function, but it often dissolves it. It can be like a light hypnotic state. It is important to be able to look at your practice with detachment. If you see what different groups do, you can put it in perspective.

If you can, discuss your practice with a teacher or other meditators. Beginners often have quite unrealistic expectations of themselves and the practice. There is a lot to learn about meditation and your own mind. Don't try to figure it out all on your own.

Teachers and experienced meditators have been there. They know what is likely to happen. Sometimes it is not at all obvious. What appears good may be useless and vice versa. Achaan Chaa, the great Thai teacher, said some students are like people in a chicken yard who ignore the eggs and pick up the droppings.

Even experienced students need help occasionally. If your practice is too solitary, you can go seriously off the rails. Shakespeare said, 'The devil can quote scripture to his purpose.' Similarly, meditation can be used badly.

In a few people, meditation can amplify their neuroses or a tendency towards excessive introspection. Meditators often get stuck in their head trips, like everyone else, but in a meditative way. A friend who was a monk for many years in Thailand said of his fellow monks: 'After all those years of meditation, most of them still don't look happy.'

When seeking out meditation groups in your neighbourhood, don't be too starry-eyed. The average Tibetan monk is no wiser or more saintly than the average Christian minister. The Buddhist and Hindu institutions themselves are little changed since the Middle Ages, and have the unthinking sexism and belief in authority so common in older cultures.

Unfortunately, if you want quality in teaching, you can't completely avoid these traditional sources. I generally find Westerners are better teachers than those from the East. Unless they have been trained in the Eastern traditions, however, their understanding of meditation can be superficial.

Go on Retreats

The best combination of people and place is a retreat. You can relax the moment you walk in the gate. The disturbances of home and work are miles away.

A retreat is a place to be, not to do. Just being able to watch yourself, without interruptions, for a weekend, can have profound effects. Without doing anything, you understand and accept yourself more fully. The body and mind have a chance to rest and repair themselves fully.

There are retreats and retreats. Some are completely silent, except for the teacher giving instructions and the odd sermon. Some are run like military camps. Others are laissez-faire — you do what you want. Some retreats isolate you from others. Some use the group spirit to accelerate the process. Some forbid exercise, some encourage it, and so on.

The popular ten-day Vipassana retreats encourage lots of meditation and 'just watching' what arises. They often alternate sitting and walking meditations, of forty-five minutes or an hour each. Zen retreats have a similar approach. They tend to be more tightly structured, with shorter but more frequent sittings.

Western teachers usually have a more humane, and less military, approach than the Eastern teachers. Many Western teachers are also psychologists and counsellors (and women!). They know the Victorian boarding school approach can be counterproductive.

Tibetan Buddhist and Christian retreats are usually more verbal, and loosely structured, involving contemplation of spiritual ideas. The Hindu-based retreats often have a more ecstatic emotional tone, stimulated by devotional singing.

I have led about forty retreats now. Because I am a participant as well as the teacher, I organise the schedule to suit myself. We have half-hour sittings alternating with half-hour sessions of yoga, walking or swimming, right through the day. Attendance at all of these is voluntary. Because this schedule helps the body become healthy and supple, I find sitting meditations improve as well.

I like silence as a general rule, personal interviews during the day and a collective reporting at night. I find it useful for people to articulate what is happening for them — it is a kind of 'naming'. By hearing what is happening for others, they can step back and see the overall patterns of change than happen on a retreat.

Retreats are good for everyone. They can be like primary school or finishing school. Beginners learn the ropes while experienced people go deep. At some stage, you know what meditation is all about. When back in the world, you will know what to aim for.

Use Tapes and Books

If you are in Perth, you can come to the Perth Meditation Centre. If not, you can buy the entire Basic Meditation Course on tape. This series consists of explanations of, and guidance through, the main meditations that we do. For further details, contact us at the address listed at the beginning of this book. Or just find us in the phone book.

Keep an eye on the bookshops. By mid-1999, my next book, on meditation and healing, will be published. It will be complementary to this one, and just as practical. You can get both books by mail order from us.

It is not easy to find good books on meditation. The books that emphasise technique alone seem to miss something. Books from a Buddhist or Hindu background often mix meditation with devotional practices or religious ideas. Those from a Western perspective are often thin on technique and rely more on inspirational or motivational ideas.

There is only one book I can recommend without reservation. It is Jack Kornfield's *A Path with Heart* (Bantam Books), subtitled 'A guide through the perils and promises of the spiritual path'. It is comprehensive, wise, witty and a pleasure to read.

SPOT MEDITATION: SLOWING DOWN

We often do things with unnecessary tension. If you are worried about work, you brush your teeth with nervous jerky movements. In this practice, you notice how you are moving, and move just 3 per cent slower. Don't believe that voice that says: 'You'll be late if you don't hurry!'

Instructions

Take some simple activity you can usually do automatically. It could be washing the dishes, feeding the dog, ironing, making a cup of tea, getting dressed, having a shower or getting into your car. It could be as brief as reaching up to a cupboard, opening it, taking something out and closing the door again.

Notice how you are moving. Just do it just a fraction slower than usual. Let your breathing be loose. Move more smoothly and deliberately.

SPOT MEDITATION: 'AM I RELAXED?'

Being relaxed means pacing yourself. It mean using just the right amount of energy for the task at hand. We could be tense at a meeting, or relaxed at a meeting. We could be tense or relaxed walking down the street or eating lunch. We don't get more things done by being tense. That is an illusion. We just get more exhausted.

Instructions

This is the shortest meditation in this book. In any activity during the day — driving, eating, walking, working, talking — ask yourself 'Am I relaxed?'

Often you will find the mind is hectic, the body is tense and you are holding your breath. You are tenser than you need to be. As soon as you notice this, you can release it. Ten seconds, and a deep breath or two, is all you need to start relaxing.

Index